The Heritage Book 1992

Edna McCann

Maxwell Macmillan Canada

Maxwell Macmillan Canada
1200 Eglinton Avenue East, Suite 200
Don Mills, Ontario   M3C 3N1

ISBN 02.954022.4

Printed and bound in Canada

Sixteenth Edition

PICTURE CREDITS

This is the sixteenth time that I have written *The Heritage Book*. I remember finishing the very first *Heritage Book*, and thinking that I would probably never do it again. But thanks to the wonderful support of my delightful readers, I find myself already preparing the seventeenth edition!

Over the years, I've received a lot of encouragement from friends, family, and acquaintances, and they often comment on the surprising freshness of the material in *The Heritage Book*. But lately this comment has been followed by the question, "How do you continue, after all this time, to find so many new stories, anecdotes, and words of wisdom?" I smile whenever someone asks me this, because, if anything, I find it difficult to decide just which anecdote or word of wisdom I will share—there are so many of them!

Writing this book through the last sixteen years has given me a real appreciation of life's remarkable novelty. As my family grows, and my friends and I "mature," I rejoice in the wonderful new experiences that we share. I'm very thankful for this opportunity to share them with all of you, too.

Edna McCann

January

O N this, the first day of a new year, I thank
the unknown author for these verses from
the poem "Starting Anew."

I will start anew this morning
With a higher, fairer creed;
I will cease to sit complaining
Of my ruthless neighbour's greed;

I will try to find contentment
In the paths that I must tread;
I will cease to have resentment
When another moves ahead.

I will not be swayed by envy
When my rival's strength is shown;
I will not deny his merit,
But I'll strive to prove my own;

I will try to see the beauty
Spread before me rain or shine;
I will cease to preach your duty,
And be more concerned with mine.

THURSDAY — JANUARY 2

IT hardly seems possible that we are starting a new year. The old adage "time flies" becomes more true with each passing year.

One of the most important lessons I have learned as I grow older is that time does indeed pass quickly, and it is important that we not waste any of it. This is not to say that we must rush about frenetically "doing" things. Indeed, some of the nicest parts of my days are spent in quiet reading or in letter-writing to my good friends. "Wasted" time is spent in worrying about things that cannot be changed, or in "envy" time wishing for what another has.

Benjamin Franklin expressed it well when he said "Dost thou love life? Then do not squander time, for that is the stuff life is made of."

FRIDAY — JANUARY 3

NEVER meet trouble halfway. Let it travel the full distance. Something usually happens to it before it arrives.

THE HERITAGE BOOK

TODAY was a beautiful winter's day. My daughter Marg, her husband Bruce, and I decided to take advantage of the weather and drive through the sunny countryside.

So early this morning we filled a few thermos jugs with hot beef stew and steaming coffee. We put some fresh buttered rolls and hunks of cheddar cheese into a large wicker picnic hamper, and with everything packed into the warm car we set off to see some of Mother Nature's glorious winter handiwork.

Instead of heading north as we often do, we set off in the direction of Niagara Falls.

It has been many years since I have seen the beauty of the falls in the winter, and the sight of the massive ice floes and ice-covered branches of the surrounding trees was truly breathtaking. Niagara Falls is considered to be a summer tourist attraction, but to me it is even more spectacular in the winter.

We picnicked at Niagara-on-the-Lake, which seems like a ghost town in the winter, and then leisurely drove home.

It was truly a wonderful winter afternoon!

THE HERITAGE BOOK

JESUS was born in Bethlehem in Judea, in the reign of Herod. After his birth, astrologers from the east arrived, asking, "Where is the child that is born to be king of the Jews?"

There is a prophecy that says, "Bethlehem in the land of Judah, you are far from least in the eyes of the rulers of Judah, for out of you shall come a leader to be the shepherd of my people."

—Matthew 2:1-2, 5-6

TODAY is Epiphany—the manifestation of Christ to the Gentiles.

The star, which the astrologers had seen at its rising, went ahead of them until it stopped above the place where the child lay. At the sight of the star they were overjoyed. Entering, they saw the child with Mary his mother and they bowed to the ground in homage of him. Then they opened their treasures and offered him gifts: gold, frankincense, and myrrh.

—Matthew 2:9-11

TUESDAY — JANUARY 7

My good friend Jake Frampton joined me for dinner this evening. Jake is one of those rare treasures: a true friend with whom you are totally comfortable, who is always there for you in good times and bad, and who is a pleasure to be with at any time.

As we enjoyed our dinner, Jake remarked that he once read "Skimming the Cream" by Zula Bennington Greene, and that our meal together had brought back her words.

"Some feel honoured when they are put at the table where the best linen and china are laid. But the ones who are really honoured are those who are set at a table where the dishes don't match and the eating utensils are recruited from the kitchen. They are the true and trusted friends who do not need to be complimented or impressed and who would never think of criticizing."

WEDNESDAY — JANUARY 8

Adversity makes men remember God.

—Livy

THE HERITAGE BOOK

My grandson Marshall works with a young Chinese-Canadian man at a law firm in Toronto. Marshall and his wife Jamie and Michael and his wife Sue-Yen have spent many pleasant evenings together, and as a result Marshall and Jamie have learned much about Chinese culture.

Last evening's encounter was no exception. The young people were discussing New Year's resolutions, which led Michael to explain the Chinese Zodiac.

The Chinese Zodiac consists of a 12-year cycle. Each year is named after a different animal that imparts to the year its distinct characteristics. Many Chinese believe that the year of a person's birth is the primary factor in determining that person's personality traits, physical and mental attributes, and degree of success and happiness throughout his or her lifetime.

This year, 1992, is the year of the Monkey. People born in this year are very intelligent and able to influence people; they are good politicians; they thirst for knowledge; they are talented and inventive; but they are easily discouraged. They seek a Dragon or a Rat.

Friday — January 10

Right is right, even if everyone is against it; wrong is wrong, even if everyone is for it.

Saturday — January 11

The darkest hour of a man's life is when he sits down to plan how to get money without earning it.

—Horace Greeley

Sunday — January 12

Sing to the Lord a new song
For he has done marvellous things.
He remembers his mercy and faithfulness to
the house of Israel.
And all the ends of the earth have seen the victory of our God.

—Psalm 98:1,3

THE HERITAGE BOOK

O NE of the most common difficulties facing those of us in the "seniors" category is a troubled financial outlook. Even those of us who thought we had planned well for our retirement years could never have foreseen an economy as it exists in this country today. As a result, many of us who are on fixed incomes are finding it more and more difficult to make ends meet.

I am in the fortunate position of being able to live with my daughter and son-in-law in a usually harmonious situation. Other of my friends are not so lucky.

One of my good friends, Mabel Stewart, decided to do something about her situation. It was with trepidation, but grim determination, that Mabel went to the local McDonald's restaurant and applied for membership in the "McMasters Program." This is McDonald's program of hiring and training seniors to work at their restaurants.

"Edna, I never thought that things could work this well. My hours are flexible; I get meal discounts while I'm working, a free uniform, paid breaks, and much more. Most of all, Edna, I'm making ends meet and I'm meeting people who keep me feeling young!"

TUESDAY — JANUARY 14

"WHAT is your age?" asked the magistrate. "Remember that you are under oath," he cautioned.

"I am twenty-one years and some months," the lady answered.

"How many months?"

Straight-faced, the woman answered: "One-hundred and eight."

WEDNESDAY — JANUARY 15

THIS is the birthdate of Dr. Martin Luther King Jr., the American clergyman and militant, non-violent civil rights leader. The late Dr. King was instrumental in introducing the strategy of civil disobedience to the black struggle for equality, and in turning the struggle into a mass movement.

Dr. King's epitaph expresses the fundamentally religious vision that was the underlying principle of his activism. On his tombstone is inscribed, "Free at last, free at last, thank God almighty I'm free at last."

<u>THURSDAY — JANUARY 16</u>

HUMAN sorrow springs from three things: to want before it is due; to want more than your share; to want what belongs to others.

—*Abdullah Ansari*

<u>FRIDAY — JANUARY 17</u>

WHEN you prevent me from doing anything I want to do, that is persecution; but when I prevent you from doing anything you want to do, that is law, order, and morals.

—*George Bernard Shaw*

<u>SATURDAY — JANUARY 18</u>

KIND words, cheerful smiles, and helping hands are shafts of sunshine through clouds of sorrow.

—*William Arthur Ward*

SUNDAY — JANUARY 19

THE harvest of the Spirit is love, joy, peace, patience, kindness, goodness, fidelity, gentleness, and self-control. There is no law dealing with such things.

—Galatians 5:22-23

MONDAY — JANUARY 20

WHAT is a friend? A single soul dwelling in two bodies.

—Aristotle

TUESDAY — JANUARY 21

A PATIENT arrived at the doctor's office and rolled up his pant leg to reveal several cuts and bruises on his shin.

"Hockey or football?" asked the doctor.

"Bridge," answered the patient.

THE HERITAGE BOOK

TODAY's weather reminded me of several verses from Thomas Noël's poem, "Old Winter."

Old Winter sad, in snowy clad,
Is making a doleful din;
But let him howl, till he crack his jowl,
We will not let him in.

Aye, let him lift from the billowy drift
His hoary haggard form,
And scowly stand, with his wrinkled hand
Outstretching to the storm.

Let his baleful breath shed blight and death
On herb and flower and tree;
And brooks and ponds in crystal bonds
Bind fast, but what care we?

Let him gnaw, forsooth, with his freezing tooth,
On our roof tiles, till he tire;
But we care not a whit, as we jovial sit
Before our blazing fire.

THE HERITAGE BOOK

How many of you have found yourselves baffled by today's latest "doublespeak" phrases—phrases carefully crafted to disguise what they really mean? At dinner last night my granddaughter Phyllis and her husband Bill kept us all in stitches as they came up with "doublespeaks," one after the other.

Here are a few of the phrases I most enjoyed:

A pencil is "a portable, hand-held communications inscriber."

A traffic light is "an electronically-adjusted colour-coded vehicular flow device."

A toothpick is "a wooden interdental stimulator."

A tent is "a frame-supported tension structure."

If you don't understand "doublespeak," don't consider yourself a failure—just an "incomplete success."

THE HERITAGE BOOK

A survey is when I ask everyone in the elevator. An in-depth survey is when I go home and ask my wife.

—*Jay Sharps*

ROBERT Burns wrote many wonderful lines, but on this, his birthday, I chose my favourites to share with you.

O, my luve's like a red, red rose,
That's newly sprung in June;
O, my luve's like the melodie
That's sweetly played in tune.

As fair art thou, my bonnie lass,
So deep in luve am I;
And I will luve thee still, my dear,
Till a' the seas gang dry.

Till a' the seas gang dry, my dear,
And the rocks melt wi' the sun:
O I will luve thee still, my dear,
While the sands o' life shall run.

SUNDAY — JANUARY 26

IF a man should do something wrong, my brother, on a sudden impulse, you who are endowed with the Spirit must set him right again, very gently.

Look to yourself, each one of you: you may be tempted too. Help one another to carry these heavy loads and in this way you will fulfil the law of Christ.

—*Galatians 6:1-2*

MONDAY — JANUARY 27

MY grandson told me this story. I found it very amusing.

A young man was hired to work for a large supermarket chain. He reported to work on a Monday morning and was warmly greeted by the store manager, who handed him a broom.

"Your first job," said the manager, "will be to sweep out the store."

"But I'm a college graduate," the young man replied.

"Oh, I'm sorry, I didn't realize," said the manager. "Here, give me the broom and I'll demonstrate."

THE HERITAGE BOOK

My sister Sarah has lived her whole adult life alone, never having found any man that she loved enough to want to share her life with. So it was to my great surprise that, during our phone conversation this evening, Sarah announced rather casually, "Oh by the way, Edna, I'm getting married next month. I hope you'll be able to come."

Such was my shock that it was some time before I was able to stammer, "Married . . . you . . . married . . . good gracious . . . who?"

Sarah sounded totally normal and calm as she told me about Richard, a retired fisherman, a widower, and a friend for years.

"We've been friends forever, Edna. Richard thought he'd never marry again, he loved his wife so much, and I'd given up any thoughts of marriage, but this seems like the right thing to do."

I will be there with bells on!

THE HERITAGE BOOK

TAKE a chance! All life is a chance. The man who goes furthest is generally the one who is willing to do and dare. The "sure thing" boat never gets far from shore.

—Dale Carnegie

AGE is like a mountain high,
Rare is the air, and blue;
A long, hard climb and
A little fatigue
But oh! what a beautiful view.

—Author unknown

STORMY weather is what man needs from time to time to remind him he's not really in charge of anything.

—Bill Vaughan

February

I THANK the unknown author for these lovely thoughts.

Nature

I am part of Nature.
I am part of everything that lives.
I am bound together with all living things in air, in land, in water.
My life depends on its resources and upon the continuity of both.
To destroy them is to destroy myself.
As a member of the human race, I am responsible for its survival.
I am a part of Nature.
I will not destroy it.

Sunday — February 2

Since we live by the Spirit, let us follow the Spirit's lead. Let us never be boastful, or challenging, or jealous toward one another.

—Galatians 5:25-26

Monday — February 3

Yesterday was officially "Groundhog Day." The "weatherman," more commonly called "Wiarton Willie," poked his head out of his snow-covered hole and, in seeing his shadow, has predicted for us another six weeks of winter.

If Candlemas Day be fair and bright
Winter will have another flight;
But if it be dark with clouds and rain,
Winter is gone and will not come again.

Whether you look to the tradition of Candlemas Day or Groundhog Day, it seems that we could be in for more of our winter-like weather.

THE HERITAGE BOOK

My sister Sarah's wedding is fast approaching. Saturday, February 22nd is the date that she and Richard have chosen for this happy event, and many of our family will be making the journey east to help celebrate the occasion. Sarah has asked that I be her matron of honour, and I am thrilled to be a part of this wonderful day in her life.

As young women, we would often lie in bed at night and talk about how we wanted our weddings to be. Sarah, ever practical and sensible, had decided that a small and quiet wedding would be to her liking, while I, the romantic, wanted everything to be "flowers and lace." I was a young woman of eighteen when George and I had our truly beautiful wedding, and it was everything I had imagined and hoped for.

Although Sarah has waited many more years for her special day, she too is having the wedding of her dreams. She and Richard have chosen to be married in the local church with only family and very close friends invited.

Her wedding "dress" will be a beautiful suit "that I will be able to wear again, Edna."

No matter her age—she sounds like an excited young girl again. I rejoice in her happiness.

THE HERITAGE BOOK

"THE bitterness of cheap quality remains long after the sweetness of low price is forgotten."

How true this is! My daughter Julia was made only too aware of this proverb in her recent purchase of a new refrigerator.

Julia is a busy executive with a large Canadian firm and as such she does much travelling around the world. Her time at home, therefore, is rather limited, and when she decided that a new refrigerator was a "must," she spent one Saturday going from store to store looking at various makes and models of this expensive appliance. Finally she found one to her liking, and the salesperson sealed the deal by offering a price that was $200.00 less than the others she had seen.

It was duly delivered but, since then, it has caused no end of problems. The first time Julia was out of town the freezer failed to freeze, and when she arrived home her frozen food was a sloppy, smelly mess. Soon after that the door seal needed to be replaced, and just last week the ice machine began churning ice non-stop.

Julia has returned the refrigerator and is now looking for a new one—hopefully of top quality.

THURSDAY — FEBRUARY 6

SMALL kindnesses, small courtesies, small considerations, habitually practised as our social intercourse, give a greater charm to the character than the display of great talents and accomplishments.

—*M. A. Ketty*

FRIDAY — FEBRUARY 7

GOD will not ask thy race,
Nor will He ask thy birth;
Alone He will demand of thee,
What hast thou done on earth?

—*Persian proverb*

SATURDAY — FEBRUARY 8

HUMOROUS alternatives to brisk walking:

1. jogging your memory
2. stretching your imagination
3. passing the buck
4. running amuck
5. pushing your luck
6. bending over backwards
7. running around in circles
8. beating around the bush

THE HERITAGE BOOK

LET us never tire of doing good, for if we do not slacken our efforts, we shall in due time reap our harvest. Therefore, as opportunity offers, let us work for the good of all, especially members of the household of the faith.
—*Galatians 6:9-10*

MONDAY — FEBRUARY 10

MY friend Mavis wrote to me from Winnipeg this week. She had been invited by a good friend to attend her grandchild's music recital at a nearby conservatory.

As Mavis and her friend made themselves comfortable, the first children came out to play a piano duet. When the two children began to play, Mavis's friend leaned over and remarked, "Well, thank goodness for this! Most places let them play one at a time and the concerts go on forever. This teacher certainly has the right idea!"

Mavis couldn't help but laugh.

TUESDAY — FEBRUARY 11

NOSTALGIA is like an anaesthetic; you experience no pain, only a beautiful haze. When you grow older, what matters to you is not the way it was but the way you remember it.

—Roger and Natalie Whittaker

WEDNESDAY — FEBRUARY 12

IN the old days there were angels who came and took men by the hand, and led them away from the city of destruction. We see no white-winged angels now. But yet men are led away from threatening destruction; a hand is put into theirs, which leads them forth gently toward a calm, bright land; so that they look no more backward; and the hand may be a little child's.

THURSDAY — FEBRUARY 13

DO not wish to be anything but what you are, and try to be that perfectly.

—St. Francis de Sales

THE HERITAGE BOOK

THIS is a special day, when we do all manner of special things for our loved ones. I recently found this anonymous piece of writing called "The Difficulty of Loving." I hope you agree that these thoughts are appropriate for us all.

God, you tell us to love. To love people and to love you.

Sometimes it is easy. The whole world seems to sing, and we look at strangers and those close to us, and our hearts smile. But it isn't always easy. Even—or particularly—with those closest to us. Where needs cry out and hurts go deep, there is more chance for things to get tangled. We mean too much to each other, and we cannot express it.

O God, help us to see clearly when nothing is clear, to speak in love when feeling unloved, and to have the wisdom and patience to speak the right words.

Tell a special Valentine how much you care.

THE HERITAGE BOOK

EVERY heart that has been strong and cheerful has left hopeful impulse behind it in the world, and bettered the tradition of mankind.

—Robert Louis Stevenson

THERE are three things that last forever: Faith, Hope, and Love; but the greatest of these is Love.

—1 Corinthians 13:13

I DESIRE so to conduct the affairs of this administration, that if, at the end, when I have come to lay down the reins of power, I have lost every other friend on earth, I shall at least have one friend left, and that friend shall be down inside of me.

—Abraham Lincoln

FAITH is the bird that fells the light and sings when the dawn is still dark.

THE HERITAGE BOOK

I FLEW from Toronto to the east coast today, in preparation for my sister's wedding on Saturday. As we winged our way eastward, I couldn't help but marvel at the technological advances that allow us to travel such great distances in just a few short hours.

I was also most favourably impressed with the flight attendant who was working in our area of the plane. Ours was a full flight, and there were a number of small children on board, several of whom were quite rambunctious. This young woman had a most delightful manner as she gave the youngsters crayons, games, stereo headphones, and other interesting things to ensure they stayed seated and quietly amused. At the same time, she was able to serve beverages to the rest of us, smiling and calm all the while.

I wonder if Orville and Wilbur Wright could ever have envisioned the airline industry as it is today. I know that if they had, they would have hired our flight attendant. It's a pleasure to see a job so well done.

THE HERITAGE BOOK

IT has been a real delight for me to spend time with Sarah and Richard. The two of them radiate happiness and their joy is contagious. The friends and relatives who are helping with the wedding arrangements are doing a wonderful job, and every time they see Sarah or Richard they give them wonderful happy smiles, obviously pleased that they are part of an elderly couple's happiness.

I still have a hard time imagining that my sister is marrying. When I see her with Richard it's as if they are celebrating their anniversary, not their wedding. They seem to share that comfortable kind of love that comes after years of happiness together.

As Sarah put it, "It's almost as if I have been married to Richard for years. Perhaps it's because being with him is how I imagined marriage to be. The friendship, the kindness—all that I've wanted I have found in the relationship that Richard and I share."

My fondest wish for them is many years of shared happiness together.

H E is happiest be he king or peasant, who finds peace at home.

—*Goethe*

O N this, my sister's wedding day, I offer ideas about love.

Love is the master key that opens the gates of happiness.

—*Oliver Wendell Holmes*

A loving heart is the truest wisdom.

—*Charles Dickens*

Love spends his all and still hath store.

—*Philip James Bailey*

Love is the enchanted dawn of every heart.

—*Alphonse de Lamartine*

To love is to find pleasure in the happiness of the person loved.

—*Gottfried Wilhelm von Liebnitz*

THE HERITAGE BOOK

To sum up, my friend: when you meet for worship, each of you contribute a hymn, some instruction, some revelation, an ecstatic utterance, or the interpretation of such an utterance. All these must aim at one thing: to build up the church.

—1 Corinthians 14:26

SARAH and Richard's wedding was truly beautiful. The church was decorated with dozens of candles and their flickering light gave a warm, soft glow to the whole ceremony.

The reception dinner was delicious, the speeches amusing (and often touching), and it was truly one of the most enjoyable days of my life.

How I wish that my husband George might have been there Saturday. However, I have a feeling that he was watching over us and enjoying every minute.

TUESDAY — FEBRUARY 25

EVERYBODY, everywhere seeks
happiness, it's true.
But finding it and keeping it
   seems difficult to do,
Difficult because we think
   that happiness is found
Only in the places where
   wealth and fame abound.
And so we go on searching
   in "palaces of pleasure"
Seeking recognition
   and monetary treasure,
Unaware that happiness
   is just "a state of mind"
Within the reach of everyone
   who takes time to be kind.
For in making others happy
   we will be happy too,
For the happiness you give away
   returns to "shine on you."

—Helen Steiner Rice

WEDNESDAY — FEBRUARY 26

IT is with our judgement as with our watches.
No two are just alike, yet each believes his
own.

—Alexander Pope

THE HERITAGE BOOK

THURSDAY — FEBRUARY 27

Lovely as it was to be away, nothing is nicer than coming home. There is such comfort in one's own bed and one's own well-known sofa or chair. Perhaps it is a factor of growing old, but each time I am away home seems just that much more inviting when I return.

FRIDAY — FEBRUARY 28

In this year of the Olympic Games, we are indeed privileged that the marvel of television enables us to see the athletic competitions as if we were there.

Although almost all of the athletes are superbly trained in their field, I must admit that I still have a soft spot in my heart for Eddie Edwards, a ski-jumper from England. This young man came to the 1988 Calgary Olympics with little skill, and even less finesse, but with much determination.

Each jump was a heart-stopping spectacle, but his fortitude earned him the nickname "the Eagle."

I think there was a little of us all in Eddie "the Eagle."

THE HERITAGE BOOK

THIS is the one year in four when we have an extra day. My husband George felt that since this day was a "bonus" we should use it especially well.

Perhaps it could be used in a special way to enrich this world. We could give the gift of love to someone special; or we could visit someone who needs companionship. There is no greater gift than that which we give of ourselves.

March

The Festival of St. David of Wales

O N the west coast of Wales is the Cathedral of St. David's, a relatively small cathedral but truly one of the loveliest in Britain. It is surrounded by the historic ruins of a very early monastery and the remnants of an earlier cathedral. There is much to learn about this legendary Welsh saint, and no trip to Wales would be complete without a visit to St. David's.

For any of my Welsh readers, I wish you a happy St. David's Day.

MONDAY — MARCH 2

I AM very fond of the month of March. I believe this is because it heralds the arrival of spring and the end, we hope, of the snow and cold weather.

Marg and I decided to find ourselves a little bit of premature spring today. At our local mall, the Horticultural Society had a magnificent display of spring flowers.

There were daffodils, tulips, hyacinths, and crocuses in all their beautiful colours. Seeing such beauty put spring in our minds and in our steps.

TUESDAY — MARCH 3

I F you want to stay young, associate with young people; if you want to feel your age, try to keep up with them.

WEDNESDAY — MARCH 4

Ash Wednesday

THE Wednesdays in Lent, seven in number, provide a wonderful opportunity to renew our faith. It is a time for all of us to recall the importance of what we learned as children but may have forgotten over the years.

I am suggesting that we renew the ten basic commandments that were given to our forebears as a basis of daily living. These "laws" of life help to keep us steadfast in times of temptation and trouble.

The commandments are simple and straightforward and perhaps their "re-discovery" would help a society that seems to have lost its way.

God spoke these words and said, "I am the Lord thy God. Thou shalt have none other god but me."

THE HERITAGE BOOK

MANY years ago, when it was rare for a woman to work outside the home, the man of the family would occasionally ask, "What do you do all day?" My friend Mavis had the perfect answer.

One day her husband returned from work to find the whole house a dreadful mess. Astounded, he quickly asked Mavis, "What in heaven's name happened here?"

"You're always wondering what I do all day—well today I didn't do it."

She was never asked the question again.

THE world judges you by what you have done, not by what you have started out to do; by what you have completed, not by what you have begun.

IT takes only a moment to hug a child but a lifetime is often too short for him to forget it.

—Tabra Malloy

THE HERITAGE BOOK

THE hymns of our faith are often the greatest influence and most readily recalled part of our heritage. On this Sunday we sang one of my favourites.

Forty days and forty nights
Thou was fasting in the wild,
Forty days and forty nights
Tempted and yet undefiled.

Keep, O keep us Saviour dear,
Ever constant by thy side,
That with thee we may appear
At the eternal Eastertide.
—*George Hunt Smyttan*
The Hymn Book

MONDAY — MARCH 9

YESTERDAY my son-in-law Bruce celebrated his birthday. It was a lovely day, with the children and grandchildren visiting for dinner and birthday cake.

Bruce received many cards and gifts, but his favourite was the button that came with Marshall's card. In large, bright letters it said, "RESPECT ME, I'M OLD."

THE HERITAGE BOOK

ALL my life I have loved to read. Many others share this love and I offer you some of their thoughts today.

A room without books is as a body without a soul.

—Cicero

Books are the quietest and most constant of friends; they are the most accessible and wisest of counsellors, and the most patient of teachers.

—Charles W. Eliot

All good and true booklovers practise the pleasing and improving avocation of reading in bed.

—Eugene Field

Books are the treasured wealth of the world and the fit inheritance of generations and nations.

—Henry David Thoreau

I cannot live without books.

—Thomas Jefferson

2nd Wednesday in Lent

THE second commandment says, "Thou shalt not make to thyself any graven image nor the likeness of anything that is in heaven above or in the earth beneath, or in the waters under the earth. Thou shalt not bow down to them or worship them."

Is God still the central object of our loyalty and adoration? It makes one think deeply.

THURSDAY — MARCH 12

As we wait for the birth of Marshall and Jamie's first child, I have been trying to think of something special I could give in celebration. My friend Emily told me of a family tradition that sounds very appropriate. Emily's daughter writes letters to her three-year-old on a regular basis, telling her about the events and people who are a part of her life. On her birthdays, relatives and friends are asked to include a letter with any gifts. Her daughter will have a treasury of letters about her life from friends and relatives of all ages, some of whom may not be alive when she is old enough to enjoy their words of love.

FRIDAY — MARCH 13

N o doubt many of my readers are in a dither today; that is how numerous people react to "Friday the 13th."

The correct terminology for this fear is "triskaidekaphobia," a rather unruly word for what, to me, is an amusing anxiety.

Many people take this very seriously, however, and these people will probably stay home in bed with the covers pulled to the chin.

Actually, that sounds like a good idea!

SATURDAY — MARCH 14

A HABIT is something you never knew you had until you tried to quit it.

SUNDAY — MARCH 15

S WEET the moment, rich in blessing
which before the Cross I spend,
Life and health and peace possessing
    from the sinner's dying friend.
Lord in ceaseless contemplation,
    fix our hearts and eyes on thee,
Till we taste thy full salvation
    and thy unveiled glory see.

—*Walter Shirley*

THE HERITAGE BOOK

BECAUSE I believe that activity is a key to longevity, I enjoy hearing of new and different activities for the older generation.

In Kansas, a group of seniors has formed the "Overland Park Dance Troupe." These energetic dancers, in their 60's and 70's, first started tapping together in a community centre class in 1983. They became so good that they decided to perform professionally and to compete in dance competitions. They have won many trophies and are still going strong, performing in outdoor theatres and shopping malls.

As one member put it, "Before this I didn't get much exercise, but six hours of practice a week makes a great workout. I feel much healthier."

Tuesday — March 17

'Tis the day for the wearin' o' the green. On this St. Patrick's Day, I offer you the words of a man who was born in the United States but who was of Irish descent.

"With good conscience our only sure reward, with history the final judge of our deeds, let us go forth to lead the land we love, asking His blessing and His help, but knowing that here on earth God's work must truly be our own."

—*John F. Kennedy*

Wednesday — March 18

3rd Wednesday in Lent

"Thou shalt not take the name of the Lord thy God in vain: for the Lord will not hold him guiltless that taketh His name in vain."

Lord, make us conscious of all that violates your holiness. Amen.

THE HERITAGE BOOK

ANYONE who will gossip with you about someone else will gossip about you with someone else.

—Sam Ewing

THE long bright icicles in dwindling
   ranks
Dripped from the murmuring eaves
   till one by one
They fell. As if the spring had now
   begun,
The quilted snow, sun-softened to the
   core,
Loosened and shunted with a sudden
   roar
From downward roofs.

—Archibald Lampman

THE HERITAGE BOOK

Spring! A time of renewal, the beginning of new life. On this day what could be more fitting as a salute to this glorious time of year than the birth of a baby?

Marshall and Jamie phoned early this morning to announce the wonderful news: a beautiful baby girl was born to them, and both mother and daughter are doing very well (father has not yet quite recovered).

As is common now, Marshall attended the delivery of the baby and, as he put it, "It was the most moving experience of my life, Gran. This tiny, perfect human being opened her eyes and although I know she probably couldn't really see us, I felt that she was looking at Jamie and me with absolute trust. We will do everything possible to justify her trust, and the trust of a loving God that has given us so perfect a being to care for."

THE HERITAGE BOOK

WHEN I survey the wondrous Cross
On which the Prince of Glory died,
My richest gain I count but loss
And pour contempt on all my pride.

Were the whole realm of nature mine,
That were a present far too small:
Love so amazing, so divine,
Demands my soul, my life, my all.

—Isaac Watts
(based on Galatians 6:14)

I OFFER these words of James Russell Lowell
to Marshall, Jamie, and their beautiful new
daughter, my great-granddaughter.

I had a little daughter,
And she was given to me
To lead me gently backward
To the Heavenly Father's knee,
That I, by the force of nature,
Might in some dim way divine
The depth of His infinite patience
To this wayward soul of mine.

TUESDAY — MARCH 24

MORE time is wasted not in hours, but in minutes. A bucket with a small hole in the bottom gets just as empty as a bucket that is deliberately kicked over.

WEDNESDAY — MARCH 25

4th Wednesday in Lent

THE fourth commandment says, "Remember that thou keep holy the Sabbath day. In six days the Lord made heaven and earth and the sea and all that is within them and rested the seventh day. Wherefore the Lord blessed the seventh day and hallowed it."

Whatever may be your religious faith, somewhere in that heritage you will find the exhortation to keep a Sabbath day. This is the one day in seven when you are away from the normal demands of your work—a time for serious reflection upon the meaning and purpose of your life.

All of us need a Sabbath.

THURSDAY — MARCH 26

SERENITY is achieved by resolutely facing life's problems and finally realizing that for many of them, nothing can be done.

FRIDAY — MARCH 27

BIG people became big by doing what they didn't want to do, when they didn't want to do it.

SATURDAY — MARCH 28

A MAN'S worst enemy can't wish him what he thinks up for himself.

—Yiddish proverb

SUNDAY — MARCH 29

4th Sunday in Lent

I SHALL light a candle of understanding in thine heart, which shall not be put out.

—The Apocrypha
Esdras 14:25

THE HERITAGE BOOK

I WAS thrilled to see my new great-grand-daughter this weekend. With a grand-mother's pride, I must say that Bethany is the prettiest baby I have ever seen. She is small and delicate with fine features, and yet she has a wonderfully healthy look about her that is unusual in such a young baby.

If ever one doubted the existence of a Higher Being, it would be necessary only to look at a newborn child to restore one's faith.

WHATEVER poet, orator, or sage may say of it, old age is still old age.
—*Henry Wadsworth Longfellow*

April

5th Wednesday in Lent

"HONOUR thy Father and thy Mother that thy days may be long in the land which the Lord God giveth thee."

To preserve the richness of your heritage, you need to start with those who are closest and most precious to you: your family. Only then will you reach out to preserve the blessings of the past; only then will you build creatively in the present; only then will you plan for the future. A wise person must retain a consciousness of the past, present, and future. Living in the three dimensions of time will allow you to reap the fullness of life.

THE HERITAGE BOOK

<u>THURSDAY — APRIL 2</u>

SOME people treat life like a slot machine, trying to put in as little as possible and hoping to hit the jackpot. Wiser people think of life as a solid investment from which they receive in terms of what they put in.

<u>FRIDAY — APRIL 3</u>

WHENEVER I get a letter from my daughter Mary, her husband John likes to include a humorous anecdote for me. Today's letter was no exception.

A young boy and his grandmother were walking on a beach by the ocean. Suddenly, a huge wave appeared out of nowhere and swept the child out to sea. The horrified grandmother fell to her knees, raised her eyes heavenward, and begged the Lord to return her beloved grandson. And lo, another wave roared in and deposited the stunned child at his grandmother's feet.

The grandmother looked the boy over carefully. He was fine.

With an angry glance heavenward, she snapped, "When we came, he had a hat!"

THE HERITAGE BOOK

THOSE who enjoy baking bread may like to try this "sour dough" yeast batter, which gives bread that distinctive tang.

2 large mealy potatoes, peeled and halved
2 tablespoons sugar
1 package dry yeast, dissolved in 1/4 cup warm water
3 cups all-purpose flour, scoop-measured

Place potatoes in a large saucepan with water to cover. Boil gently until potatoes fall apart. Do not drain. Force through a sieve, liquid and all, and cool to room temperature. Add water (if necessary) to make 3 cups. Pour into a large bowl. Using a non-metal spoon, stir in sugar, dissolved yeast, and 2 cups flour. Beat until smooth and creamy. Cover with a tea towel and set in a warm (70°F approx.) spot to stand for 24 hours, at which time the batter should smell pleasantly sour. Add remaining flour and 1 cup warm water. Cover with the towel and let stand 2-3 days. Store the starter in the fridge in a tightly-covered container. To use the starter, stir in any surface liquid, remove what you need, and bring it to room temperature. Replenish what you remove by adding equal parts flour and water (i.e. 1 cup = 1/2 cup water + 1/2 cup flour).

SUNDAY — APRIL 5

Passion Sunday

IN the Cross of Christ I glory
Towering o'er the wrecks of time;
All the light of sacred story
Gathers round its head sublime.

When the woes of life o'ertake me,
Hope deceives and fears annoy;
Never shall the Cross forsake me
As it glows with peace and joy.

Bane the blessing, pain and pleasure
By the Cross are sanctified,
Peace is there that knows no measure
Joys that through all time abide.
                              —*John Bowering*

MONDAY — APRIL 6

WHEN the day returns, call us up with
morning faces and with morning hearts,
eager to labour, happy if happiness be our por-
tion and if the day be marked for sorrow,
strong to endure.
                              —*Robert Louis Stevenson*

TUESDAY — APRIL 7

OPPORTUNITIES are never lost. The other person takes those you miss.

WEDNESDAY — APRIL 8

6th Wednesday in Lent

THESE commandments provide the basic laws for individuals living in society:

Thou shalt do no murder.
Thou shalt not commit adultery.
Thou shalt not steal.
Thou shalt not bear false witness against thy neighbour.

THURSDAY — APRIL 9

KIND words are the music of the world. They have a power which seems to be beyond natural causes, as though they were some angel's song which had lost its way and come to earth.

—*Frederick William Faber*

FRIDAY — APRIL 10

IF you have a clear conscience and good health, if you have a few good friends and a happy home, if your heart has kept its youth and your soul its honesty, then cheer up—you are one of life's fortunate millionaires.

SATURDAY — APRIL 11

I WAS delighted to see a robin in our back yard this morning. This harbinger of spring was a most welcome sight! Perhaps I hadn't been watching closely enough, but this robin is the first I have seen since last fall.

I have always found the subject of bird migration fascinating. How do they know when to leave? How do they know when to return? If the weather stays warm in the south why don't they just stay there?

My friend Emily, who winters in Florida, is quite sure she has the answers to these questions.

"The birds just watch the retirees from the north. When they pack up and head south in the fall, the birds follow their cars; and they know it's time to return north when the same thing happens in the spring."

Palm Sunday

Lift high the cross, the love of Christ pro-
claim
Till all the world adore his sacred name.
Come, brethren, follow where our captain
trod,
Our King victorious, Christ the Son of God.
Lift high the cross
O Lord, once lifted on the glorious tree
As thou hast promised, draw men unto thee.
Lift high the cross
So shall our song of triumph be
Praise to the crucified for Victory.
—*George William Kitchen*

THE HERITAGE BOOK

MEMORIES are marvellous things. Memories allow us to relive the most wonderful times of our lives again and again. Memories can keep us feeling young. I hope you enjoy "The Heart Remembers" from Patience Strong.

The heart remembers everything
Although the mind forgets—
The raptures and the agonies,
The hopes and the regrets.
The heart remembers April
When the snows of winter fall—
Hearing on the bitter wind
The sweetest song of all.
When Youth has had its shining hour
And Love its golden day,
Time may fade the colours
And the glory turn to gray;
But something of the magic lingers,
Never to depart,
Deep down in the secret places of
   the quiet heart.

TUESDAY — APRIL 14

My brother Ben is an avid gardener, and spring always finds him in the local hardware stores picking up odds and ends and the occasional new small gardening tool.

For many years, these trips to the store would take the better part of two hours.

"The trips are much shorter now," laughed his wife Marie. "Ben used to stand and wait at the counter for a salesperson to arrive. This could often take some considerable time. Now when he goes to the store, he stands near the large and expensive tractor lawn mowers and 'ums' and 'ahs' with what appears to be great interest.

"In no time at all, Edna, a salesperson arrives at his side and then Ben asks for what he really came for. It works every time!"

WEDNESDAY — APRIL 15

Wednesday of the Holy Week

"Thou shalt not covet thy neighbour's house, thou shalt not covet thy neighbour's wife, nor his servant, nor his maid, nor his ox, nor his ass, nor anything that is his."

THE HERITAGE BOOK

I SPOTTED this note on a church newsletter: "The Lord loveth a cheerful giver. He also accepteth from a grouch."

Good Friday

A LMIGHTY God, look graciously we pray, on this your family for whom our Lord, Jesus Christ, was willing to be betrayed and given into the hands of sinners and to suffer death upon the Cross, who now lives and reigns with you and the Holy Spirit, One God for ever and ever. Amen.

—The Book of Common Prayer

W HEN you say a situation or a person is hopeless, you are slamming the door in the face of God.

—Charles Allen

THE HERITAGE BOOK

Easter Sunday

CHRIST is risen from the dead and become the first fruits of them that slept. For since by man came death, by man came also the resurrection of the Dead.

On this day the Lord has acted,
We will rejoice and be glad in it.

Thanks be to God, who giveth us the victory
through our Lord, Jesus Christ.

Jesus Christ is risen today. Alleluia!
He is risen indeed. Alleluia!

A Happy Easter to All!

MONDAY — APRIL 20

FOR me, Easter is the loveliest day of the year. The spiritual "lift" I get from the Easter service leaves me with a sense of renewed strength of faith, and of the purpose of life on this earth and the belief in the life to come.

When my husband George was alive, his Easter service was always the finest of the year. He seemed able to give to the entire congregation so much of his own vibrant spiritual faith that, without exception, each person who heard him had their own faith renewed and their spirits lifted. I hope each of you had the same wonderful day that we in our family did.

TUESDAY — APRIL 21

OUR old family doctor once told me, "You will never know how your children have turned out until your grandchildren are grown."

THE HERITAGE BOOK

I AM not afraid of tomorrow, for I have seen yesterday and I love today.

THURSDAY — APRIL 23

M Y son-in-law Bruce came home with a wonderful surprise for Marg. She was intrigued, of course, and quickly went out to the garage where he had put the surprise. There in the garage were two beautiful brand-new bicycles—his and hers.

Bruce explained, "A few weeks ago I bumped into an old friend, Ian Brown. Ian was the coach of the Canadian cycling team for many years, and so is extremely knowledgeable about all aspects of cycling. He and his family live in Ottawa, and there they own the 'Ottawa Bikeway,' a store specializing in quality bicycles and accessories. When I told Ian I was considering buying bikes for you and me, he couldn't have been more helpful. He recommended the proper size, type, and model most suited to our needs. As well, he recommended helmets and clothing. He had all of what we needed delivered to my office this morning. I hope that on the first nice day we can go for a countryside tour."

FRIDAY — APRIL 24

B EING poor is a problem, but being rich isn't necessarily the answer.

SATURDAY — APRIL 25

I ENJOY this story about George Bernard Shaw:

An autograph collector sent a photo of George Bernard Shaw to the author requesting that he sign and return the picture.

Instead, he received a snappy note of refusal from Shaw's secretary.

Undeterred, the collector sent another photo with the following explanation: "I have no personal interest whatsoever in possessing George Bernard Shaw's autograph. I wish to obtain it so that I may sell it for a profit."

Shaw returned the photo, autographed. The note with it said, "Bravo! Such honesty deserves encouragement."

SUNDAY — APRIL 26

S ING to the Lord; bless his name; announce his salvation, day after day.

—Psalm 96:2

MONDAY — APRIL 27

THIS morning I received a parcel in the mail marked "Fragile." It came from my good friend Mavis who lives in Winnipeg, and contained several jars of Mavis's special home-made chili sauce.

Naturally, I was very happy to receive her delicious chili sauce, but I was also very interested in the way she had packed the jars for shipment. Instead of the styrofoam "peanuts" or shredded newspaper that was once so popular, Mavis had filled the box with popcorn. It worked perfectly, and it can also be thrown out in the back yard to feed the birds.

At a time when we all need to think about what we can be doing to save our planet, it's nice to see how innovative people can be.

TUESDAY — APRIL 28

SELF-CONFIDENCE is the first requisite to great undertakings.

—Samuel Johnson

D ON'T be afraid to take a big step if one is indicated. You can't cross a chasm in two small jumps.

—David Lloyd George

April Showers

T HE leaves are fresh after the rain,
The air is cool and clear,
The sun is shining warm again,
The sparrows hopping in the lane
Are brisk and full of cheer.

And that is why we dance and play,
And that is why we sing,
Calling out in voices gay,
We will not go to school today
Nor learn anything!

It is a happy thing, I say,
To be alive on such a day.

—James Stephens

May

WE who were born
In country places
Far from cities
And shifting faces,
We have a birthright
No man can sell,
And a secret joy
No man can tell.

Pride of trees,
Swiftness of streams,
Magic of frost
Have shaped our dreams.
No baser vision
Their spirit fills
Who walk by right
On the naked hills.

—*Eiluned Lewis*
from "Dew on the Grass"

SATURDAY — MAY 2

POVERTY is caused by many things—like having two children in university at the same time.

SUNDAY — MAY 3

I AM the good shepherd; I know my own sheep and my sheep know me—as the Father knows me and I know the Father—and I lay down my life for the sheep. But there are other sheep of mine, not belonging to the fold, whom I must bring in, and they will listen to my voice. There will then be one flock, one shepherd.

—John 10:14-16

MONDAY — MAY 4

A MAN who has committed a mistake and does not correct it is committing another mistake.

—Confucius

THE HERITAGE BOOK

IN the words of Martin Luther, "Everything that is done in the world is done by hope."

To be hopeful is to enjoy all of life, in good times and in bad. Here is what some people feel about hope:

The word which God has written on the brow of every man is "Hope."

—Victor Hugo

Hope ever urges us on, and tells us tomorrow will be better.

—Albius Tibullus

Hope is the dream of a waking man.

—Diogenes

Hope is like the sun, which, as we journey toward it, casts the shadow of our burden behind us.

—Samuel Smiles

True hope is swift and flies with swallows' wings;
Kings it makes gods, and meaner creatures kings.

—William Shakespeare

THE HERITAGE BOOK

ALTHOUGH I have never watched a great deal of television, I very much enjoy the show "Murder She Wrote," starring Angela Lansbury as mystery writer Jessica Fletcher. My granddaughter Phyllis watches it regularly and has taped many of the programs for me. Now, on a rainy day, I will often choose to watch one of the hour-long cassettes.

I think the reason I enjoy the show so much lies in the ability of its star, Angela Lansbury.

Born in London, England, Angela emigrated with her family in 1940 to New York where she enrolled in drama school. At sixteen she moved to Los Angeles, and at eighteen she was under contract to M.G.M. studios. In 1949, she married Peter Shaw and they eventually had two children, a boy and a girl.

During the 1960's Angela played in many long-running Broadway plays, including "Mame." It was in the 1980's, however, with the television show "Murder She Wrote," that her career really took off. With her boundless energy, optimism, and healthy, attractive good looks, Angela Lansbury has shown the world that "women of a certain age" can accomplish great things.

Thursday — May 7

The bad thing about good things is that they come to an end, and the good thing about bad things is that they also end.

Friday — May 8

As we head into this year's baseball season, I confess I have become a "dyed in the wool" Blue Jays fan. I follow "our boys'" games regularly on radio and television, and on a few occasions each season I am fortunate enough to see a game live at the SkyDome.

Although the skills of all of the players are to be admired, it is the ability of the catchers that I find truly amazing. These men crouch fearlessly behind the plate as the pitcher launches the ball towards them at speeds of nearly a hundred miles per hour.

I was surprised to learn that before 1875 the catchers played barehanded, and that it often took a platoon of catchers to finish a game. In 1875, in a game against Harvard, William McGunnigle of Fall River, Massachusetts wore a pair of bricklayer's gloves, and thus spawned the use of the heavily padded gloves so necessary in today's game.

SATURDAY — MAY 9

THIS is a wonderful day for those of us who live in southern Ontario to visit the neighbourhood parks or public gardens.

The growth and development of these gardens in the last twenty years has been phenomenal. Many of the towns and cities near lakes or rivers have set aside small tracts of land for public use, and the beauty of the gardens can be often quite breathtaking.

The month of May sees tulips of every colour in abundance, along with the beautiful yellow daffodils. Later in the month, the lilacs' colour and perfume fill the air. Each week another type of flower seems to take over and fill in the spaces.

These gardens are well worth a weekly visit.

SUNDAY — MAY 10

Mother's Day

SHE was as good as goodness is,
Her acts and all her words were kind,
And high above all memories
I hold the beauty of her mind.
——*Frederic Hentz Adams*

THE HERITAGE BOOK

IN 43 B.C., Cicero wrote the following six Mistakes of Man. I think you will agree that they are as relevant today as they were then.

1. The delusion that individual advancement is made by crushing others.

2. The tendency to worry about things that cannot be changed or corrected.

3. Insisting that a thing is impossible because we ourselves cannot accomplish it.

4. Refusing to set aside trivial preferences.

5. Neglecting development and refinement of mind, and not acquiring habits of reading and studying.

6. Attempting to compel other people to believe and live as we do.

TUESDAY — MAY 12

IT is not only what we do, but also what we do not do, for which we are accountable.

WEDNESDAY — MAY 13

MY mind lets go a thousand things
Like dates of wars and deaths of kings,
And yet recalls the very hour—
'Twas noon by yonder village tower,
And on the last blue moon in May—
The wind came briskly up this way,
Crisping the brook beside the road;
Then, pausing here, set down its load
Of pine-scents, and shook listlessly
Two petals from that wild-rose tree.
                    —*Thomas Bailey Adrich*

THURSDAY — MAY 14

THE people who have "all the luck" are those who don't depend on it.

THE HERITAGE BOOK

DIGGING trenches for asparagus is good for the muscles and waiting for the plants to settle teaches patience to those who are usually in too much of a hurry.

—*Miriam Waddington*

MY grandson Geoffrey has an excellent answer for those people who ask, "What do you want to be?"

"I don't know what I want to be. Maybe they haven't even invented my job yet."

FAITH is the substance of things hoped for, the evidence of things not seen.

—*Hebrews 11:1*

THE HERITAGE BOOK

It has been a perfectly glorious day here in Muskoka. Marg, Bruce, and I have spent our traditional long weekend together opening Eleanor's cottage. Every year it seems to become an easier task.

This is mainly because cottages have become less "cottagey" and more like homes, so the usually demanding chores like painting screens and doors have given way to easier tasks like clipping in aluminum frames. Floors that often needed sanding and varnishing have been urethaned, and they shine with only a light mopping. Built-in vacuum systems allow us to dust and vacuum cottages in mere minutes. The cleaning of the "little shack out back" is no more, thanks to indoor facilities.

Many old-time cottagers bemoan the modern changes, and extol the virtues of "rugged cottage life," which means no electricity, no running water, rustic and uncomfortable beds, damp furniture, and many types of resident insects and animals.

As I settled into a warm bed to read in the glow of my bedside lamp, I welcomed every new and labour-saving device that Eleanor's cottage provides.

TUESDAY — MAY 19

READING the fine print may give you an education—not reading it will give you experience.

WEDNESDAY — MAY 20

YOU cannot prevent the bird of sorrow from flying over your head, but you can prevent it from building nests in your hair.

—*Chinese proverb*

THURSDAY — MAY 21

AT this time of year many schools have their annual commencement. At one such event, at Middlebury College in the U.S., Alistair Cook remarked, "There's a very odd tradition in this country which dictates, especially around commencement time, that someone who's tottering downhill will be able to tell people walking uphill what is over the top of the hill."

THE HERITAGE BOOK

CHRISTIE, a good friend of my granddaughter Phyllis, has been teaching for a number of years. A friend gave this amusing list to Christie. We all enjoyed it—I hope you will too.

You know you have been teaching too long when:

— the new vice-principal says, "Hi! You taught me in grade three"
— you ask the people beside you at the movie theatre some questions about the movie, just to make sure they're watching
— you tell your dinner guests to put their hands on their heads when they are ready for dessert
— while reading the latest novel, you make a list of good questions to ask
— you return your friend's letters with grammar, spelling, and handwriting corrected.

SATURDAY — MAY 23

IN prosperity, our friends know us; in adversity, we know our friends.

SUNDAY — MAY 24

"COME and have breakfast," Jesus addressed his disciples. They knew it was the Lord Jesus as they saw him take the bread and fish and break it and give it to them.

This (writes John), makes the third time that Jesus appeared to his disciples after the resurrection from the dead.

—paraphrased from John 21:13-14

MONDAY — MAY 25

YESTERDAY was the birthdate of Queen Victoria of England. Not only was Victoria England's longest-reigning monarch, she was also one of the most beloved. As my girls used to say, "You'd love somebody too, if their birthday gave you a holiday."

TUESDAY — MAY 26

A VERY dear friend of mine passed away on the weekend. At such a time it is often difficult to know what to say to the family that has been left to sorrow.

Grace Noll Crowell wrote this lovely poem that I passed on to Bill's widow, Louise, today.

Let me come in where you are weeping, friend,
And let me take your hand.
I, who have known a sorrow such as yours,
Can understand.
Let me come in—I would be very still
Beside you in your grief;
I would not bid you cease your weeping, friend,
Tears bring relief.
Let me come in—I would only breathe a prayer,
And hold your hand,
For I have known a sorrow such as yours,
And understand.

WEDNESDAY — MAY 27

R EAL security is based on wanting less—not having more.

Ascension Day

ALLELUIA! Alleluia! Like the sun from
out the wave
He has risen
  up in triumph
From the darkness of the grave;
He's the splendour of the nation
He's the lamp of endless day
He's the very Lord of glory
Who has risen up today!

—*The Hymn Book*

FRIDAY — MAY 29

THE wearer of smiles and the bearer of a kindly disposition needs no introduction but is welcome anywhere.

—O. S. Marden

SATURDAY — MAY 30

NOT many things are harder to tolerate than the annoyance of a good example.

SUNDAY — MAY 31

GOD is our refuge and strength, a very present help in trouble.

—Psalm 46:1

June

My husband George and I were married on this day, and to the memory of our happy life together I offer this poem about friendship.

A friend is like a golden gift
That makes the whole day brighter,
A friend can give a little lift
That makes a burden lighter,
Life is full of lovely things
But best of all are these:
The happiness that friends can bring,
The gold of memories.

TUESDAY — JUNE 2

My daughter Julia stopped in for a visit today and she had an amusing story to tell. She had gone to the bank this morning and was using the automatic teller to make a withdrawal. She inserted her card in the usual manner, punched in the transaction, and waited. Nothing happened. She pushed the "cancel" button. The machine door promptly shut and the red "closed" sign dropped into place, but no money or card were forthcoming. Fortunately, the bank itself was open and someone was able to open the machine, retrieve the card, and provide the funds she had requested.

The woman who helped Julia thanked her for her patience, and related this story of a less patient customer in Clearwater, Florida: when the bank's automatic teller swallowed a man's card and refused to give him the money he wanted to withdraw, he pulled out a handgun and fired six shots into the machine. It still refused to give him the money.

WEDNESDAY — JUNE 3

How you play the game shows something of your character; how you lose shows all of it.

THE HERITAGE BOOK

<u>THURSDAY — JUNE 4</u>

THE world is a looking glass, and gives back to every man the reflection of his own face. Frown at it, and it in turn will look sourly upon you; laugh at it and with it, and it is a jolly, kind companion.

—*William Makepeace Thackeray*

<u>FRIDAY — JUNE 5</u>

MARG and her children Jenny and Justin dropped in for a visit this evening on their way home from the twins' soccer practice. Marg prepared some lemonade for all of us to share while we listened to the children discuss the game.

"Boy, it was great, Gran," Justin enthused. "Jed and Mike and I have this great passing play that we use and we've already scored six goals between us. We just run and run and hardly anybody can catch us we're so fast!"

"It was a great practice," Jenny agreed. "Megan wore her new hair ribbons and do you know what? They exactly match the colour of our new team shirts so I'm going to get Mommy to buy some for me, too. Megan and I will match for the next game. Oh, yes, and I scored once, too."

SATURDAY — JUNE 6

Today was a day well-spent in the garden. For the past several years, my good friend Will, an avid gardener, has come by at this time to assist with the planning and planting of our gardens. With his help, they have expanded and flourished and are truly beautiful to behold, particularly as the summer progresses and the plants grow and spread.

There is nothing nicer than to watch someone at work in the garden who truly loves being there. Each delicate plant is treated with such gentle kindness. Will actually talks to the plants while he works, explaining where they are planted and why.

"You impatiens don't want to get too much direct sunlight, so we'll put you where you'll have some afternoon shade. Geraniums, we'll put you in these big pots by the terrace."

My son-in-law Bruce used to chuckle at Will's habit of "chatting up" the plants, but the excellent results of the past few years have turned "Bruce the sceptic" into "Bruce the believer." As I wandered over to where Bruce was working, I was amused to hear him quietly whispering, "For goodness sake, this is the best I can do—try to make a good go of it— please!"

SUNDAY — JUNE 7

Pentecost

PRAISE the Lord in his sanctuary, praise him in the firmament of his strength. Praise him for his mighty deeds, praise him for his sovereign majesty. Praise him with the blast of the trumpet, praise him with lyre and harp, praise him with timbrel and dance, praise him with strings and pipe. Praise him with sounding cymbals, praise him with clanging cymbals. Let everything that has breath praise the Lord! Alleluia.

—Psalm 150

MONDAY — JUNE 8

HARRY S. Truman, late president of the United States, once remarked, "I have found the best way to give advice to your children is to find out what they want and then advise them to do it."

TUESDAY — JUNE 9

ON my birthday, I am reminded of the lines, "For all within is young and glowing, in spite of old age's outward showing."

WEDNESDAY — JUNE 10

A DAY of worry is more exhausting than a week of work.

THURSDAY — JUNE 11

THOSE men whom I have seen succeed best in life have always been cheerful and hopeful men, who went about their business with a smile on their face, and took the changes and chances of this mortal life like men, facing rough and smooth alike as it came.
—*Charles Kingsley*

FRIDAY — JUNE 12

LET mystery have its place in you; do not be always turning up your whole soil with the ploughshare of self-examination, but leave a little fallow corner in your heart ready for any seeds the wind may bring, and reserve a nook of shadow for the passing bird; keep a place in your heart for the unexpected guest, an altar for the unknown God.
—*Henri Frédéric Amiel*

THE HERITAGE BOOK

ERMA Bombeck, whose books I enjoy very much, has written many funny, insightful words about being a mother. Here she replies to the age-old children's complaint, "You don't love me!"

I loved you enough to bug you about where you were going, with whom, and what time you would get home.

I loved you enough to keep silent and let you discover that your hand-picked friend was a creep.

I loved you enough to stand over you for two hours while you cleaned your room, a job that would have taken me fifteen minutes.

I loved you enough to let you see anger, disappointment, disgust, and tears in my eyes.

I loved you enough to ignore what "every other mother" did.

I loved you enough to shove you off my lap, let go of your hand, be mute to your pleas, and insensitive to your demands—so that you had to stand alone.

I loved you enough to accept you for what you are, not what I wanted you to be.

But most of all, I loved you enough to say "no" when you hated me for it. That was the hardest part of all.

SUNDAY — JUNE 14

THE Bible is a window in this prison of hope, through which we look to eternity.

—Dwight

MONDAY — JUNE 15

WITH summer vacation nearing, many parents will be looking for activities to interest and occupy their children.

An annual event at the Canadian National Institute for the Blind is "Kidsummer Day," an opportunity for children who are able to see to get together with blind children and play, learn, and have fun.

On this day, sighted children wear blindfolds to enter the world of the blind. They play "beeping baseball" and discover that running without seeing where you are going is scary. They walk down hills with white canes and try to read books with their fingers.

They eat hot dogs and pudding and get very messy. Most of all, though, it gives sighted children an insight into the world of the blind, and offers ways to learn how to interact with them in a normal and natural way.

THE HERITAGE BOOK

THIS morn I climbed the misty hill
And roamed the pastures through;
How danced thy form before my path
Amidst the deep-eyed dew!

When the red bird spread his sable wing,
And showed his side of flame;
When the rosebud ripened to the rose,
In both I read thy name.

—Ralph Waldo Emerson

THERE is no difference between knowledge
and temperance; for he who knows what is
good and embraces it, who knows what is bad
and avoids it, is learned and temperate.

—Socrates

THE young man who has not wept is a savage, and the old man who will not laugh is
a fool.

—George Santayana

THE HERITAGE BOOK

ALL of us have said things that later proved to be very wrong. So-called "experts" are no different, and I offer these examples of some really big "goofs."

"Far too noisy, my dear Mozart. Far too many notes."
—Emperor Ferdinand of Austria, 1786
(after first hearing "The Marriage of Figaro")

"The radio craze will die out in time."
—Thomas Alva Edison, 1922

"God himself could not sink this ship."
—Titanic deckhand, April 10, 1912

"I am finished."
—Winston Churchill
(after being replaced as First Lord of the
Admiralty during W.W.I, 1915)

"For the majority of people, smoking has a beneficial effect."
—Dr. Ian G. McDonald, 1963

SATURDAY — JUNE 20

"LIKE everyone else, I feel the need of relations and friendship, of affection, of friendly intercourse, and I am not made of stone or iron, so I cannot miss these things without feeling, as does any other intelligent man, a void and deep need.

"I tell you this to let you know how much good your visit has done me."

—*Vincent Van Gogh*

SUNDAY — JUNE 21

Father's Day

IT matters not that Time has shed
His thawless snow upon your head,
For he maintains, with wondrous art,
Perpetual summer in your heart.

—*William Hamilton Hayne*

MONDAY — JUNE 22

"SING a song of summer, the world is nearly still."

I welcome with great happiness that most wonderful of seasons, summer.

TUESDAY — JUNE 23

"DEAR Margaret,
This is just a weather report.
Letter follows.
As spring follows winter.
That is to say: not immediately."
—Edna St. Vincent Millay

WEDNESDAY — JUNE 24

I READILY admit that my taste in art is very primitive. When I view a painting, I don't feel that I must guess what the painter has portrayed. The more realistic a painting is, the better I like it.

Is it any wonder then, that I enjoy the work of Norman Rockwell, Robert Bateman, Jan Vermeer, and Renoir?

I often feel badly that I don't appreciate the nuances and subtleties of many critically acclaimed artworks. Sometimes I will talk a friend into visiting a gallery with me, and I enter with every intention of seriously studying the work being presented.

As likely as not, however, some aspect of a painting will set me to chuckling, and I am forced to leave to avoid embarrassment. Perhaps humour is just a different form of appreciation.

HAPPINESS is having friends who laugh at your stories when they're not so good, and sympathize with you in your troubles when they're not so bad.

FRIDAY — JUNE 26

ALTHOUGH they are nearly a thing of the past, drive-in movies still attract the young and the old in many of the smaller communities of our country.

Young couples often bring small children in their pyjamas, and while the youngsters sleep in the back seat of the car, the parents enjoy an evening's entertainment—without the cost of a babysitter.

Drive-in theatres are not only found in North America. Some of these open-air cinemas in other lands have unusual regulations.

A notice on a wall in a village in India warns: "Viewing the show from beyond the boundary walls by sitting on a camel or in nearby trees is strictly prohibited. Additionally, the management cannot be held responsible in the event that a viewer is bitten by a scorpion or a snake."

THE HERITAGE BOOK

THIS evening we enjoyed an excellent barbecued dinner. My grandson's wife, June, brought a delicious salad of tuna fettuccine that could be a meal on its own. I present this for all of you who are recipe collectors.

1 12-oz. package fettuccine noodles
1 medium sized bunch arugula
1/4 cup + 1 tbsp. olive or salad oil
2 6-oz. jars marinated artichoke hearts
1 12.5-13 oz. can tuna, drained
1/2 teaspoon salt
1/2 teaspoon coarsely ground pepper

Begin about 2 hours before serving, or early in the day.

In a saucepan, prepare fettuccine as directed. Meanwhile, mince arugula. Drain fettuccine; set aside. In the same saucepan, over medium-high heat, cook arugula in 1 tbsp. hot olive or salad oil, stirring constantly, until wilted (about 1 minute). Remove saucepan from heat. Return fettuccine to pan; add artichoke hearts with marinade, tuna, salt, pepper, and 1/4 cup olive or salad oil. Toss. Refrigerate until chilled. Makes 6 servings.

SUNDAY — JUNE 28

LET the words of my mouth, and the meditation of my heart, be acceptable in thy sight, O Lord, my strength and my redeemer.
—Psalm 19:15

MONDAY — JUNE 29

WE often respond the way we "should" feel, rather than the way we "do" feel.

TUESDAY — JUNE 30

A SLIP of the foot you may soon recover, but a slip of the tongue you may never get over.
—Benjamin Franklin

July

Canada Day

GRANDFATHER,
Look at our brokenness.

We know that in all creation
Only the human family
Has strayed from the Sacred Way.

We know that we are the ones
Who are divided.
And we are the ones
Who must come back together
To walk in the Sacred Way.

Grandfather—Sacred One
Teach us love, compassion, and honour
That we may heal the earth
And heal each other.

—Ojibway People of Canada

THE HERITAGE BOOK

MY friend Marcia sent me this story from her home in Boston.

Ring Lardner, an American humorist, was a moody man who could suddenly become silent in the middle of a conversation. One night, while he was dining with a friend at a restaurant, he became lost in contemplation of a picture on the wall next to him. It was an old print of a horse race at Saratoga at the turn of the century. Lardner, ignoring both his dinner and his companion, stared fixedly at the print saying not a word. As his friend, respecting his silence, finished eating, Lardner finally spoke up. "You know," he said, "that jockey next to the rail isn't trying."

AS the baseball season gains momentum we are inundated with facts and figures from the game's broadcasters. My son-in-law John found this little-known baseball fact in an old book he was reading recently. The "Iron Man" of baseball is, in fact, a woman. Miss Harriet Smith of Brookline, pitching for the Hollywood Girls team in 1931, pitched 83 innings in one week, and 200 games in one playing season.

THE HERITAGE BOOK

THIS day is the "Glorious Fourth," a day of patriotic celebration for our neighbours in the United States. Here are some thoughts from famous Americans about their country.

Then join hand in hand, brave Americans all.
By uniting we stand, by dividing we fall!
—*John Dickinson*

I am not a Virginian, but an American.
—*Patrick Henry*

I was born an American; I live an American; I shall die an American.
—*Daniel Webster*

O beautiful for spacious skies,
  For amber waves of grain,
For purple mountain majesties
  Above the fruited plain!
America! America!
  God shed his grace on thee
And crown thy good with brotherhood
  From sea to shining sea.
—*Katharine Lee Bates*
"America the Beautiful"

Happy Independence Day to our American friends!

THE HERITAGE BOOK

O LORD, our God, grant us grace to desire you with our whole heart, that so desiring we may seek and find you, and so finding you, may love you, and loving you, may hate those sins from which you have redeemed us.

—Anselm

MONDAY — JULY 6

MY good friend and neighbour Lila McGuiness is an elderly widow who lives alone. Although her family visits quite regularly, distance prevents them from assisting with the daily routine of keeping house.

Because Lila suffers from angina, many chores such as vacuuming or lifting a laundry basket are too much for her. A group of us in the neighbourhood got together to discuss how we could help Lila and lighten her family's load. We have come up with a plan that I think will work well. Marg made up a calendar and each of us has signed up for various days during the next few months. We will spend some time each day with Lila doing the chores that need to be done to keep her life at home running smoothly.

It gave me great joy to see the old-time values of caring, sharing, and helping come so naturally to us all.

THE HERITAGE BOOK

IF you have endured a dull party, you will enjoy this story:

Many years ago, Alexander Woollcott and a friend were attending an extremely dull party. After about a half-hour, they could stand it no longer and made a hasty exit.

"Whew, that was boring," muttered his friend. Woolcott, in characteristic style, added, "Now that we've left, it must be ghastly!"

TIME draweth wrinkles in a fair face, but addeth fresh colours to a fast friend, which neither heat, nor cold, nor misery, nor place, nor destiny, can alter or diminish.

—*John Lyly*

THIS is a special day in our family. Phyllis and Bill celebrate the ninth anniversary of their wedding, and their twins, Justin and Jenny, celebrate their seventh birthday.

It gives me such joy to see the family grow from generation to generation.

THE HERITAGE BOOK

For many years, summer was a time for those of us who enjoyed warm weather to spend hours soaking up the sun's rays, and working hard at turning our skin a dark brown colour. The tanned look was considered to be healthy and glamorous.

In more recent years, doctors have discovered that the sun has a very damaging effect on our skin. Prolonged exposure to sunlight causes premature aging and skin cancer.

Fortunately, scientists have developed sunscreens or sunblocks that help protect our skin from the sun's rays.

In a discussion with a dermatologist, I discovered that I should wear sunscreen not only in the summer, but all year round—every time I go out in the sun. I also learned that the S.P.F. rating on lotion containers stands for "Sun Protection Factor," and the higher the number, the greater the protection. The doctor suggested that S.P.F. 15 is the lowest number that should be worn on skin exposed to the sun, and that in summer S.P.F. 45 is highly recommended.

Although it's much too late to prevent "premature" skin aging, I will feel better knowing that I am protecting my skin from further damage.

SATURDAY — JULY 11

IDEALS are like stars; you will not succeed in touching them with your hands, but like the seafaring man on the desert of waters, you choose them as your guides, and, following them, you reach your destiny.

—*Carol Shurz*

SUNDAY — JULY 12

Now that the daylight fills the sky,
We lift our hearts to God on high.
That He in all we do and say
May keep us free from harm today.

Keep Thou our inmost conscience pure
Our thoughts from foolishness secure
And help us check the pride of sense
By self-restraining abstinence.

—*John Mason Neale*

MONDAY — JULY 13

REFLECT upon your present blessings—of which every man has many—not on your past misfortunes, of which all men have some.

—*Charles Dickens*

TUESDAY — JULY 14

CONSCIENCE takes up more room than all the rest of a person's insides.

—*Mark Twain*

WEDNESDAY — JULY 15

ONE of my favourite treats in hot summer weather is an ice cream cone. Although I enjoy it all year round, ice cream is a real summer cooler on a warm evening.

According to one authority, the first ice cream was made thousands of years ago when someone accidentally left a bowl of milk outside on a cold night. Over 3000 years ago, the Chinese mixed snow and fruit juices to make desserts. In the 4th century, Alexander the Great enjoyed ice cream made from honey, fruit juices, and milk, which was frozen with snow and carried down from the mountains by relays of slaves.

Ice cream was popular in Europe in the 1500's and 1600's, and was enjoyed by well-to-do colonists in America. In 1846, an American woman named Nancy Johnson invented the hand-cranked freezer.

The progress from ice cream's beginnings to today's many flavours has been a delicious one.

THE HERITAGE BOOK

B LISS Carman wrote a beautiful poem titled "Roadside Flowers." Those who enjoy flowers on a country drive will also enjoy his words.

We are the roadside flowers,
Straying from garden grounds;
Lovers of idle hours,
Breakers of ordered bounds.

If only the earth will feed us,
If only the wind be kind,
We blossom for those who need us,
The stragglers left behind.

And lo, the Lord of the Garden,
He makes His sun rise,
And His rain to fall like pardon
On our dusty paradise.

On us He has laid the duty—
The task of the wandering breed—
To better the world with beauty,
Wherever the way may lead.

Who shall inquire of the season,
Or question the wind where it blows?
We blossom and ask no reason,
The Lord of the Garden knows.

Friday — July 17

I is not the lazy who are most inclined to prayer; those pray most who are most, and who, having worked hard, find it intolerable to be defeated.

Saturday — July 18

I have held many things in my hands, and I have lost them all; but whatever I have placed in God's hands, that I still possess.

—*Martin Luther*

Sunday — July 19

Songs of praise the angels sang,
Heaven with alleluias rang,
When creation was begun,
When God spake and it was done.

Hymns of glory, songs of praise,
Father, unto thee we raise.
Jesus, glory unto thee,
With the Spirit, ever be.

—*James Montgomery*

THE HERITAGE BOOK

IN the morning mail I received a postcard from my great-grandson Geoffrey. Geoff is at a summer camp in northern Ontario, and from his glowing report he seems to be having a splendid time. The closing line of his card certainly captured my interest, though.

"Have you ever seen a real skunk right up close?"

This leaves one to wonder . . . did he see a skunk "right up close?" How close? Was he sprayed?

Children for many years have written this type of attention-grabbing note to startled parents. My son-in-law Bruce found some amusing lines in an old magazine:

"Dear Mom and Dad: We've been taking some pretty long hikes this week. Please send my other sneaker. Love, Jimmy."

"Dear Mom: Please bring some food when you come to visit. We only get breakfast, lunch, and dinner here. Your hungry son, John."

"Dear Mother and Father: Yesterday our counsellor told us where babies come from. You lied to me. From Mary-Margaret."

THE HERITAGE BOOK

PARENTS with young children are often looking for ways to encourage their youngsters to read during summer vacations.

Local libraries usually help by running special summer programs for children. As well, our library offers extended summer hours to allow working parents time to bring their children in after dinner.

My granddaughter Phyllis has come up with a special plan to encourage Justin and Jenny to read. For each book the children finish they are given a card worth ten points. These cards may be redeemed for "treats" at any time. For example, one ten-point card may be exchanged for an ice cream cone. Three cards may be worth a dinner at a restaurant. Ten cards may be redeemed for a trip to Ontario Place.

This plan is working so well that Phyllis is having to make as many as three trips a week to the library. She is certainly not complaining about this and, in fact, some of the children's friends are asking their parents if they may start such a program in their own homes.

THE HERITAGE BOOK

A FINANCIAL genius is someone who can earn money faster than the family can spend it.

M ARG and Bruce celebrated their wedding anniversary today. Marg gave Bruce a card on which were inscribed these lovely words by Thomas à Kempis:

Love is good above all others,
which alone maketh every
burden light.
Love is watchful, and
whilst sleeping still
keeps watch; though fatigued
is not weary;
though pressed is not
forced.
Love is sincere, gentle,
strong, patient, faithful,
prudent, long-suffering,
manly.
Love is circumspect, humble,
upright, not weary, not fickle,
nor intent on vain things;
sober, chaste, steadfast,
quiet, and guarded in all the senses.

THE HERITAGE BOOK

FRIDAY — JULY 24

JUST think how happy you'd be if you lost everything you have right now—and then got it back again.

SATURDAY — JULY 25

I THINK George Bernard Shaw spoke for many of us when he described his behaviour during danger.

"In moments of crisis my nerves act in a most extraordinary way. When disaster seems imminent, my whole being is simultaneously braced to avoid it. I size up the situation in a flash, set my teeth, contract my muscles, take a firm grip of myself, and without a tremor, always do the wrong thing."

SUNDAY — JULY 26

MAKE me a clean heart, O God, and renew a right spirit within me. Cast me not away from thy presence and take not thy Holy Spirit from me.

—Psalm 51:12-13

Monday — July 27

I ENJOYED Lawrence Clarke Powell's thought on books.

"Books, I say, are truly alchemical agents; for they, more than any other of man's creations, have the power of transforming something common (you and me as we are most of the time) into something precious (you and me as God meant us to be)."

Tuesday — July 28

WHAT lies behind us and what lies before us are tiny matters compared to what lies within us.

Wednesday — July 29

YOU can do anything if you have enthusiasm. Enthusiasm is the yeast that makes your hopes rise to the stars. Enthusiasm is the sparkle in your eyes, the swing in your gait, the grip of your hand, the irresistible surge of will and energy to execute your ideas.

—Henry Ford

THURSDAY — JULY 30

WHY is it that we so often make the same mistake more than once? I chuckle when I remember what Richard Needham said in 1969: "The value of making mistakes is to learn which ones you enjoyed the most, so you can make them all over again."

FRIDAY — JULY 31

I ENJOYED a very relaxing lunch early this afternoon. I had music playing while I sat in the cool shade and sipped a tall glass of lemonade. The music was such a beautiful complement to the sunny day that I was reminded of some people's thoughts on music.

Rhythm and harmony find their way into the secret places of the soul.

—Plato

Language is sound as sense. Music is sound as sound.

—R. Murray Schafer

Music is love in search of a word.

—Sidney Lanier

August

STAR-GAZING is wonderful summer evening entertainment. As we sat outside tonight with our eyes fixed heavenward I was reminded of these words of Lord Byron:

Ye stars! which are the poetry of heaven,
If in your bright leaves we could read the fate
Of men and empires—'tis to be forgiven
That in our aspirations to be great
Our destinies o'erleap their mortal state,
And claim a kindred with you; for ye are
A beauty and a mystery, and create
In us such love and reverence from afar,
That fortune, fame, power, life, have named
    themselves a star.

THE HERITAGE BOOK

ALMIGHTY God, your son Jesus Christ fed the hungry with the bread of his life and the word of his kingdom. Renew your people with your heavenly grace. In all our weakness, sustain us by your true and living bread, who lives and reigns with you and the Holy Spirit, one God, now and forever. Amen.

TODAY I received a letter from my friend Marcia. She included a humorous list of terms for things I didn't even know were defined!

Quenby: a spot on a window that you realize is on the other side only after you've spent ten minutes trying to rub it off.

Pantrymime: making actions with your hands that resemble what you're looking for in your kitchen. For example, making cutting motions when you're trying to find a knife.

Shaffering: spraying someone with crumbs when you try to speak with a mouth full of soda crackers.

THE HERITAGE BOOK

M Y son-in-law John has started a hobby he seems to be enjoying very much: furniture refinishing. My daughter Mary, used to the frugal life of a minister's wife, began going to garage sales and picking up pieces of furniture that appeared to be well-made, but were camouflaged by layers of paint. At first, Mary would simply add another layer of paint to the object and put it to use.

One day John decided to find out what was under the paint. To his surprise, the tea wagon he had chosen turned out to be made of fine quality oak. He stripped and refinished the wagon to its original lustre and it became a focal point in their dining room.

John is quick to point out, however, that not everything is a good find. He told us about buying a crimson bureau he and Mary had thought was a "steal." He spent hours using a vile-smelling paint stripper only to find under the hideous crimson paint a layer of hideous green paint. This stripping continued until finally John was down to the wood—poor quality plywood!

WEDNESDAY — AUGUST 5

A MAN who works with his hands is a laborer; a man who works with his hands and his brain is a craftsman; a man who works with his brain and his heart is an artist.

—Louis Nizer

THURSDAY — AUGUST 6

JAMES Dent once wrote in the Charleston West Virginia Gazette, "It was one of those perfect summer days—the sun was shining, a breeze was blowing, the birds were singing, and the lawn mower was broken."

FRIDAY — AUGUST 7

TO have what we want is riches; but to be able to do without is power.

—George McDonald

SATURDAY — AUGUST 8

I AM back in Muskoka for my annual visit at the summer home of my dear friend Eleanor.

In the Northern Advocate of 1870 it was written, "Without much hazard of prophetic failure, the day may be predicted, and not far distant either, when the wealthy in our large cities will erect villas for the summer residence of the families on the healthful and enchanting shores of Lake Muskoka."

They did come, of course, both the wealthy and the not-so-wealthy, to buy land and build summer homes. Many of the original Muskoka cottages have endured through five or six generations of the same family.

As one long-time cottager has said, "It's important to have something in your life that doesn't change. For our family, it's the cottage."

SUNDAY — AUGUST 9

O GOD, help me to have victory over myself, for difficult to conquer is oneself, though when that is conquered, all is conquered.

THE HERITAGE BOOK

YESTERDAY, Eleanor and I enjoyed a morning worship service at the "Church of the Kettles" near Mortimer's Point on Lake Muskoka. This tiny church is accessible only by water, but each Sunday the church is filled with worshippers who have come by motor launch, sailboat, or canoe. The dress is casual, and the beautiful hanging flower baskets on the porch give a feeling of "hominess."

The Anglican service was traditional in format. It radiated a simplicity reminiscent of the quiet peace of a small sheltered corner in the woods.

Should you find yourself in the Muskokas I highly recommend attending a service at the "Church of the Kettles."

WHEN grace is joined with wrinkles, it is adorable. There is an unspeakable dawn in happy old age.

—Victor Hugo

THE HERITAGE BOOK

THIS beautiful poem by David Bates is a favourite of mine.

Speak Gently

Speak gently; it is better far
To rule by love than fear;
Speak gently; let no harsh words mar
The good we might do here.

Speak gently to the little child
Its love be sure to gain,
Teach it in accents soft and mild
It may not long remain.

Speak gently to the aged one,
Grieve not the careworn heart;
The sands of life are nearly run,
Let such in peace depart.

Speak gently, kindly to the poor;
Let no harsh tone be heard.
They have enough they must endure
Without an unkind word.

Speak gently to the erring; know
They must have toiled in vain;
Perchance unkindness made them so,
Oh, win them back again.

THE HERITAGE BOOK

A NEIGHBOUR of Eleanor's here at the cottage has a son who was recently hired as a pilot for a Canadian airline.

"It seems unbelievable, Eleanor," she remarked. "They don't think anything of handing him a multi-million-dollar aircraft to fly. Why, just a few years ago I was very cautious about letting him drive our family car."

I WOULD rather read slowly and explore all the dungeons and secret passages than be a speed-reader who bounds from parapet to parapet and thinks he has seen the castle.

—Jim Fiebig

Two shall be born a whole wide world apart and one day out of darkness they shall stand and read life's meaning in each other's eyes.

THE HERITAGE BOOK

ALMIGHTY God, you have broken the tyranny of sin and sent into our hearts the Spirit of your Son. Give us grace to dedicate our freedom to your service that all people may know the glorious liberty of the Children of God, through Christ Jesus our Lord.

—Collect for this Day

MONDAY — AUGUST 17

SOMETHING that I enjoy very much here in Muskoka is the summer theatre group known as the "Muskoka Festival."

The Opera House in Gravenhurst, where we enjoyed Saturday's production, opened on March 12, 1901, with a revue called "The Days of the Year." It was a community showplace, with a wood-beamed ceiling, stained glass windows, and twin brass chandeliers (costing only $50.00 each).

Back in 1965 the Opera House was nearly demolished in order to make way for a shopping mall. But Gordon Sloan (of Sloan's Restaurant fame) led a group to save and restore the historic building.

Now, these many years later, cottagers and tourists are enjoying summer stock theatre in this old Muskoka institution.

THE HERITAGE BOOK

WE have been enjoying the fresh fruits and vegetables of the season. Is there anything more delicious than a tomato sandwich made from slices of freshly-picked, vine-ripened tomatoes?

My favourite of the many types available is the "beefsteak" tomato, a large and very flavourful fruit that usually requires only one slice to make a whole sandwich.

Another interesting variety is the "cherry 100's" which grow, much as grapes do, in bunches. They may be eaten as a snack, or as an excellent addition to a summer salad.

No matter which you prefer, this is certainly the time to enjoy these delicious fruits.

THE "good old days" were never that good, believe me. The good new days are today, and better days are coming tomorrow. Our greatest days are still unsung.

—*Hubert Humphrey*
former U.S. Vice-President

Thursday — August 20

THERE is no beautifier of complexion, or form, or behaviour, like the wish to scatter joy, and not pain, around us.

—Ralph Waldo Emerson

Friday — August 21

THE great countryside bathed in golden sleep,
The trees, the bees, the soft peace
  everywhere—
I think of the cow's tail, how all summer long
It beats the shapes of harps in the air.

—Oscar Williams

Saturday — August 22

IT seems to me we can never give up longing and wishing while we are thoroughly alive. There are certain things we feel to be beautiful and good, and we must hunger after them.

—George Eliot

THE HERITAGE BOOK

SUMMER suns are glowing over land and sea
Happy light is flowing bountiful and free
Everything rejoices in the mellow rays
All earth's thousand voices swell the psalm of
  praise.
God's mercy streameth over all the world,
And his banner gleameth everywhere unfurled
Broad and deep and glorious as the heaven
  above
Shine in might victorious his eternal love.
—Bishop Walsham How
The Hymn Book

ON my first evening back home from
Muskoka, Marg, Bruce, and I went for a
long walk down to the millpond.

I am always surprised at this time of year to
notice that the days are becoming shorter and,
as this evening, there is a slight cooling in the
night air.

How quickly the summers seem to pass.
Perhaps it is my age showing when I say that
the winters seem much longer and the summer days fly by.

TUESDAY — AUGUST 25

My son-in-law John has a friend in the ministry who works between two parishes. He holds a 9:00 a.m. service at one church and then he drives the few miles to his next church for an 11:00 a.m. service. The parking lot is often full, so John's friend is left to find a parking spot some distance away from the church, and then quickly hike back. He came up with an ingenious solution to this problem by placing a sign on one spot in the lot that reads, "You Park—You Preach."

WEDNESDAY — AUGUST 26

The test of first-rate intelligence is the ability to hold two opposed ideas in mind at the same time and still retain the ability to function. One should, for example, be able to see that things are hopeless and yet be determined to make them otherwise.

—*F. Scott Fitzgerald*

THURSDAY — AUGUST 27

Success consists in getting up just one more time than you fall.

THE HERITAGE BOOK

O NE of our neighbours, a young man, is entering his first year of university this fall. He looks forward to this change in his life with great eagerness and with just a touch of nervousness.

In the mail this morning he received confirmation of his room in residence, his roommate's name, and a number of other letters and documents designed to make his first few days at school run as smoothly as possible.

However, his favourite message was a typed sheet that read the following:

Before I came to university, I sure wish I'd known:

— that I would change so much and barely realize it
— that you were smart in high school? So what!
— that you can know everything and fail a test
— that you can know nothing and pass a test
— that home would be a great place to visit
— that change is a very positive experience and shouldn't be avoided
— that friendships are what makes university worthwhile.

THE HERITAGE BOOK

SUMMER is a necklace set with fragrances from many common things: wild grape, black locust, honeysuckle, freshly mowed sweet clover; elderberries blooming in masses of tiny, creamy white flowers that greet you with their delicate, fruity smell even before you see them. And growing corn just about when the silks show. There are leaves to sniff: bergamot, geranium, dill, sage, penny royal. There are fruits—early apples, fresh strawberries. Or watermelon, stabbed with a butcher knife so that the rind splits ahead of the knife and the watermelon smell rushes out to meet you.

One of summer's best fragrances is the smell of rain when the first big drops come slowly down and sink into the grateful hot earth or onto hot, dry stones. If peace has a fragrance, it is the fragrance of this rain.

—Rachel Pedden

MAY the Father of our Lord Jesus Christ enlighten the eyes of our hearts, that we may know what is the hope to which he called us.

—Ephesians 1:17-18

THE HERITAGE BOOK

THIS piece of writing, by Goethe's mother, is one of my favourites.

I rejoice in my life because the lamp still
   glows;
I seek no thorny ways;
I love the small pleasures of life.
If the doors are too low, I bend;
If I can remove a stone from the path, I do so;
If it is too heavy, I go round it.
I find something in every day that pleases me.
The cornerstone, my belief in God, makes my
   heart glad and my face shining.

September

Our gardens seem to be at their peak of beauty this week. This is an appropriate day for the poem "My Garden."

A Garden is a lovesome thing, God wot!
Rose plot,
Fringed pool,
Fern'd grot—
The veriest school
Of peace; and yet the fool
Contends that God is not—
Not God! in gardens! when the eve is cool?
Nay, but I have a sign;
'Tis very sure God walks in mine.
                    —*Thomas Edward Brown*

THE HERITAGE BOOK

My good friend Jake stopped in this evening to tell us about his vacation. He spent last week with his friend John in New York State on the "Seaway Trail." This is the route that parallels New York State's freshwater shoreline from Ripley, on Lake Erie, to Rooseveltown, on the St. Lawrence River.

For Jake, visiting several of the lighthouses along the route was a very interesting part of their trip. During the colonial period in the U.S., each of the thirteen colonies had been responsible for its own navigational aids. But on August 7, 1789, Congress passed the Federal Lighthouse Act, putting into motion the construction, maintenance, and administration of hundreds of structures. Over twenty of these would protect vessels navigating the waterways adjacent to the Seaway Trail.

The architectural styles of the lighthouses range from High Victorian Gothic (as in the Dunkirk Lighthouse), to rustic turn-of-the-century Shingle Style.

Although some of the lighthouses are private residences, many of the others have been restored and are now open to the public as fine museums. Each one is so different in style and history that Jake and John felt visiting each was a unique experience.

THURSDAY — SEPTEMBER 3

H ENRY David Thoreau, during a week-long trip on the Concord River, wrote:

"The wilderness is near as well as dear to every man. Even the oldest villages are indebted to the border of wild wood which surrounds them, more than to the gardens of men. There is something indescribably inspiriting and beautiful in the aspect of the forest skirting and occasionally jutting into the midst of new towns, which, like the sand-heaps of fresh fox-burrows, have sprung up in their midst. The very uprightness of the pines and maples asserts the ancient rectitude and vigour of nature. Our lives need the relief of such a background, where the pine flourishes and the jay still screams."

Perhaps the development of our towns and cities might have been different if the planners and developers had read these wise words from Thoreau.

FRIDAY — SEPTEMBER 4

A LMOST everyone intends to accomplish something worthwhile—as soon as there is time.

THE HERITAGE BOOK

Our learning usually passes through three stages: first we learn the right answers; then we learn the right questions; and finally, we learn which questions are worth asking.

O God, in the course of this busy life, give us times of refreshment and peace; and grant that we may so use our leisure to rebuild our bodies and renew our minds that our spirits may be opened to the goodness of your creation through Jesus Christ, our Lord.

—Book of Alternative Services

Labour Day

Labours accomplished are pleasant.

—Cicero

No labour is difficult if you wish to do it.

—St. Jerome

THE HERITAGE BOOK

IN most areas of our province children are returning to the highly anticipated first day of school. Many youngsters are more than happy to return, as it is a chance for them to see old friends and compare summer experiences. Others are not quite as eager. New students to the area are often shy, and fearful of "never" making new friends.

A friend of my granddaughter Phyllis teaches a grade seven class, and she has a good technique for dealing with the "what will I do if nobody talks to me" problem. She gives each student a sheet of paper, at the top of which is written, "You must find someone who . . . ." Underneath are listed a series of statements such as "plays hockey," or "loves to ski," or "has two pets," etc. The object of the exercise is to ask these questions of different people in the room. When students have found a person that "plays hockey," for example, that person signs their name beside the statement. A person may sign a sheet only once, so the students must find at least twenty different people to fill each sheet. The first student with a full sheet wins a prize. This exercise is lots of fun for the children, and a wonderful "ice-breaker."

THE HERITAGE BOOK

My grandson Fred and his wife June have always had a magnificent rose garden. Recently, a good friend gave June a recipe for rose potpourri, taken from a diary kept by the wife of a 19th-century sea captain.

Ingredients:
A Chinese jar, an apron full of rose petals, a handful of salt, two ounces of whole allspice (crushed), two ounces of stick cinnamon (broken in pieces), one ounce of orris root (bruised and broken), two ounces of lavender flowers, eight drops of oil of rose, 1/4 pint of cologne (whatever you can afford).
Directions:
Gather the roses when all the dew is gone. Separate the petals and let them dry. Then scatter them in a large covered dish and sprinkle each layer with salt. Stir every morning for ten days. Let them stand for six weeks in a covered fruit jar with the allspice and cinnamon at the bottom. When you put them in the Chinese jar, add the orris root, the lavender, the rose oil, and the cologne.

A proper potpourri will last for years and years. All you have to do is add a little lavender, or rose oil, whenever you wish—and cologne when you can spare it.

THE HERITAGE BOOK

ONE should not marry to find happiness but to share happiness.

As the first week of school comes to a close I am reminded of this poem by Enola Chamberlain.

When September Comes

It is September now, and school has started.
The bells are gay, but I am heavy-hearted.
For you, who were a babe but yesterday,
Have gripped a pencil, started on your way.
To learn the things the world would have you
    know;
To pick, yourself, the path where you must go.

Now I am no longer your all in all,
But just your starting point . . . the heart-high
    wall
From which you leap to enter on your
    flight . . .
God grant your skies be calm and blue and
    bright.
I would not have you stay, the gift of years
Is yours, but still I shed these foolish tears.

THE HERITAGE BOOK

A COMPLIMENT is verbal sunshine.

THE things, good Lord, that I pray for, give me grace to labour for.

—*St. Thomas More*

THE more a man finds his sources of pleasure in himself, the happier he will be.

—*Arthur Schopenhauer*

THE HERITAGE BOOK

M ANY times a day I realize how much my own outer and inner life is built upon the labours of my fellow men, both living and dead, and how earnestly I must exert myself in order to give in return as much as I have received.

—Albert Einstein

O N my walk today I was surprised to see how many of the leaves have changed colour. The big old maple tree at the edge of the millpond is a stunning shade of crimson. It seems as if it were only last week that Marg and I were on a walk and seeing signs of spring in the buds on this tree—and now its leaves are falling.

The flaming hills of autumn
Are a wonder to behold.
When all the countryside
Turns to red and gold.

THE HERITAGE BOOK

MY good friends Will and Muriel stopped in this evening and, as often happens, our conversation turned to grandchildren. Will and Muriel had just returned from a week of babysitting two of their younger grandchildren, a boy of four and a girl of two. Will told me the story:

"On the whole, I think it went pretty well. The children were quiet, well-behaved, obedient—and then their parents left.

"As the door closed, Alison collapsed to the floor in a wailing heap, pausing only momentarily to yell 'Mommeee, Daddeee.' Muriel managed to pick up her tiny, hollering little body and restore some calm with a twenty-minute rock in the rocking chair.

"Brian, meanwhile, attempting to show his 'maturity,' managed to bolt himself into the bathroom, and I was forced to gain entry by removing the entire doorknob and lock system.

"On day two, both children woke up in the morning with small spots on their chest, much like mosquito bites. Within a few hours, new spots were appearing all over their bodies, and I knew it wasn't mosquito bites. Both of them had the chicken pox!

"All in all—it was a pretty normal week, Edna."

FRIDAY — SEPTEMBER 18

RESOURCES of the spirit are like savings; they must be accumulated before they are needed.

SATURDAY — SEPTEMBER 19

THE goal of science is to describe the universe; the goal of religion is to find the most abundant life which man may possess in such a universe.

—*Kirtley F. Mather*

SUNDAY — SEPTEMBER 20

ABIDE with us, O Lord, for it is toward evening and the day is far spent; abide with us and with the whole church. Abide with us in the evening of the day, in the evening of life, in the evening of this world. Abide with us and with all the faithful ones, O Lord, in time and in eternity.

—*Lutheran Manual of Prayer*

Autumn Flight

Now the wild geese are going over,
Clanking their chains on the windless sky,
Over the cornfields, over the clover,
Shouting their wild exuberant cry:
"Come with us, come with us—come"

They are calling,
And I, with no answer shaped in my mouth,
Stand where the painted leaves are falling,
Watching them disappear in the south,

Disappear from my sight and hearing,
Going to who knows what far land,
Straight as an arrow, and not fearing
The journey ahead. . . .

I lift my hand
Bidding them to stay their avid going
Across the wide and uncharted track,
Calling to them, and yet well knowing
That only the spring will bring them back.
                              —*Grace Noll Crowell*

Welcome, Autumn!

TUESDAY — SEPTEMBER 22

W E have all enough strength to bear other people's troubles.
—Duc de la Rochefoucauld

WEDNESDAY — SEPTEMBER 23

A s the baseball season heads into its final weeks, I found it interesting to hear these comments from a radio sportscaster about players and their salaries:

"Many players in the game today are making multi-millions of dollars, and yet they will often appear to be disinterested or distracted and some will seem to be not trying.

"One highly-paid player for a west-coast team was quoted as saying that it's hard to get 'up' for some games. This man came from lowly circumstances, is not well-educated, lives a lifestyle that most people would never dare to dream of, and all that he has to do to earn his living is to work for about eight months a year. It seems difficult to imagine that this would not be sufficient inspiration to be 'up' for a game."

Thursday — September 24

No man or woman can really be strong, gentle, pure, and good without the world being better for it, without someone being helped and comforted by the very existence of that goodness.

—Phillips Brooks

Friday — September 25

When one has much to put in them, a day has a hundred pockets.

—Friedrich Nietzsche

Saturday — September 26

Perfection is finally attained, not when there is no longer anything to add, but when there is no longer anything to take away.

—Antoine de St. Exupery

SUNDAY — SEPTEMBER 27

MAY God support us all the day long, till the shades lengthen and the evening come and the busy world is hushed and the fever of life is over and our work is done—then in His mercy may He give us a safe lodging and a holy rest and peace at the last.

—John Henry Newman

MONDAY — SEPTEMBER 28

WE like someone because. We love someone although.

TUESDAY — SEPTEMBER 29

To be without some of the things you want is an indispensable part of happiness.

WEDNESDAY — SEPTEMBER 30

THE hush of autumn holds the land in peaceful, quiet rest.

October

IN autumn, breezes cool,
Mark the end of summer's rule . . .
Fragrant mow and laden bin,
Prove the harvest's gathered in.

Shorter day and longer night,
Winging birds in homeward flight
Haze of blue the woods enfold,
Falling maples red and gold.

In autumn, colour flares
From the bounty nature spares . . .
Richer, brighter still it glows
Than midsummer ever shows.

And the crickets mournfully
Sing of winter soon to be . . .
Light the lamp and close the door,
Summer's gone its way once more.

—Elsie Grant

FRIDAY — OCTOBER 2

ONE of the most practical things we can do with our holidays and leisure time is to store our minds with pictures of beauty and truth. By discriminating thought, conversation, and observation, we may lay up hidden sources of strength and grace.

SATURDAY — OCTOBER 3

AT this time of year I enjoy visiting any one of the many fall fairs in my area. Although some of the fairs have taken on modern additions (elaborate midways, expensive "junk food" stands, etc.), others in the more rural areas maintain their original fair traditions.

At the fair we attended today we were able to see the Pet Show, with prizes for the Most Beautiful, Largest, Smallest, Most Unusual, and Friendliest Pets. We watched as young 4H Club members showed with pride the animals they had raised.

We saw prize-winning pumpkins, squash, jams, pies, and a host of other culinary delights.

The highlight of the day was the magnificent dinner provided by the Ladies Auxiliary. It was a wonderful way to spend a fall Saturday.

THE HERITAGE BOOK

SUNDAY — OCTOBER 4

Now thank we all our God,
With heart, hands, and voices,
Who wondrous things hath done,
In whom His world rejoices;
Who from our mother's arms
Hath blessed us on our way
With countless gifts of love,
And still is ours today.

—Rev. Martin Rinkart

MONDAY — OCTOBER 5

No man ever distinguished himself who
could not bear to be laughed at.

—Maria Edgeworth

TUESDAY — OCTOBER 6

Fall, leaves, fall; die flowers away:
Lengthen night and shorten day:
Every leaf speaks bliss to me,
Fluttering from the autumn tree.

—Emily Brontë

THE HERITAGE BOOK

IT's when you're safe at home that you wish you were having an adventure. When you're having an adventure, you wish you were safe at home.

—Thornton Wilder

JAKE and I had a very interesting discussion this evening. We had been listening to the baseball game when, in frustration, Jake turned off the radio with a disgusted snort.

"It's absolutely no wonder at all that children aren't able to speak the English language correctly today," he said. "When children hear announcers saying, 'He hit that ball real good,' or 'He run that base like his feet was hurting,' they assume that this form of speech is acceptable and correct."

We agreed that it must be very difficult for children to know how to speak well. It is not only radio or television personalities who have fallen prey to the debasement of the language—people in all walks of life and various levels of education seem to have forgotten (or never learned) the rules of grammar. For those of us who admire good English this is a torment to the ear.

FRIDAY — OCTOBER 9

FORGIVE what you can't excuse.

—*Mary Wortley Montagu*

SATURDAY — OCTOBER 10

OUR family is gathering together for this Thanksgiving weekend. Next to the Christmas holiday, this is the occasion of our largest family gathering of the year. Perhaps it is because we have so much to be thankful for that we all enjoy this happy time.

Sarah and Richard arrived last night from the east coast and are looking forward to their first family Thanksgiving together.

For flowers that bloom about our feet;
For tender grass so fresh and sweet;
For song of bird and hum of bee;
For all things fair we hear and see,
Father in Heaven we thank Thee.

—*Ralph Waldo Emerson*

THE HERITAGE BOOK

Honour the Lord with thy substance and with the first fruits of all thine increase, so shall thy barns be filled with plenty and thy presses shall burst out with new wine.

—Proverbs 3:9-10

MONDAY — OCTOBER 12

Thanksgiving Day

As we sat at the festive table this evening I remembered my first Thanksgiving as a young bride. My husband George and I had invited the whole family over for dinner. As often happens, when you most want things to go well is exactly the time they don't.

The turkey was overcooked, the vegetables were undercooked, and the pumpkin pies were just short of dreadful. People were very kind, however, and managed to eat enough so that I considered the dinner a success.

As is our custom after dinner, each person stood and told us of one thing they were thankful for. My young cousin John summed it up nicely for everyone as he stood and proclaimed, "I'm thankful that I don't have to eat Edna's cooking every day!"

TUESDAY — OCTOBER 13

ITALIAN movie director Vittorio de Sica once remarked, "If there is one great truth I have learned about life, it is this—never cry over anything that can't cry over you."

WEDNESDAY — OCTOBER 14

OF all the advances in the field of technology, none is more awesome than the computer.

Interestingly, the father of the modern computer industry, Herman Hollerith, showed little promise of great things as a child. He once jumped out of a school window to avoid writing a spelling test. At Columbia University he did poorly in bookkeeping and mechanics, two of the basics of computer science.

The turning point for Hollerith came in 1887 when he devised a punch-card information-processing machine for the U.S. Census Office. Called "statistical pianos" by some, these machines were fast and accurate. Processing the raw data from the 1890 census, the machines calculated a population of 63 million (later proven accurate).

His Tabulating Machine Company was one of the three that formed the Computer Tabulating Recording Company in 1911, later becoming I.B.M.

THURSDAY — OCTOBER 15

HOSPITALITY doesn't depend on size or supply. If the heart is big enough, so is the table and so is the house.

FRIDAY — OCTOBER 16

WORRY is the interest paid by those who borrow trouble.

—George Washington Lyon

SATURDAY — OCTOBER 17

BOOKS are the legacies that a great genius leaves to mankind, which are handed down from generation to generation, as presents to the posterity of those who are yet unborn.

—Joseph Addison

SUNDAY — OCTOBER 18

I SHALL seek to develop the perfection of generosity, virtue, doing without, wisdom, energy, forbearance, resolution, love, serenity.

—Buddhist Spirituality

THE HERITAGE BOOK

B LESSED is he who speaks a kind word; thrice blessed is he who repeats it.
—*Arabian proverb*

MARG and I went shopping today. Although we were looking for an anniversary gift for friends, we found Christmas gifts for Justin, Jenny, and Bethany.

It is early to be doing any Christmas shopping, but we both found this idea to be too good to pass by: we have ordered a personalized book for each child.

These books are created with the help of a computer program and a laser printer. There are a number of different stories, but each book centres on a theme that makes the child a hero. Their name, age, birthplace, and the names of a few friends and family members are placed in the computer, and within minutes the printed story pages come flipping out, ready to be bound in a pre-designed hard cover.

We are picking up our books tomorrow—how I wish it were soon to be Christmas!

THE HERITAGE BOOK

MY friend Emily sent me a lovely note telling me of her latest travel experiences. Over the last two weeks she has been roaming about in New England, staying in various inns and "bed-and-breakfast" homes. Although she enjoyed all of the inns, her favourite was the Fitzwilliam Inn at Fitzwilliam, New Hampshire.

"This has been a charming New England inn since it was built in 1796. Just six miles north of the Massachusetts border, it overlooks the town common and has a lovely view of Mt. Monadnock. The inn is beautifully decorated with antiques, and the plaster walls are outlined with 200-year-old hand stencilling.

"Fitzwilliam is noted for being the antique centre of New Hampshire, and the browsing is a delight.

"The food is delicious, and is served in front of a blazing fire in the fireplace. Many traditional New England dishes are offered along with homemade breads and desserts.

"If you have the chance, Edna, this is a wonderful and charming place to visit for a night— or a week."

THE HERITAGE BOOK

THERE is only one way to get ready for immortality, and that is to love this life and live it as bravely, and faithfully, and cheerfully as we can.

—*Henry Van Dyke*

GIVE me the gladsome autumn,
Show me the leaves at play. . . .
The beauty of October,
In vibrant colour display.

THERE is a time to be born, and a time to die, says Solomon, and it is the memento of a truly wise man; but there is an interval between these two times of infinite importance.

—*Richmond*

THE HERITAGE BOOK

G OD of constant love, you have guided your people in all times and ages. May we who offer you our praise today always be ready to follow where you lead. We ask this in the name of Jesus Christ our Lord. Amen.

—Book of Alternative Service

MONDAY — OCTOBER 26

O NE of the things I most enjoy in this season is making chili sauce, spaghetti sauce, and the many other delights that come from fresh tomatoes.

Actually, we were very late in arranging a time that we all found to be convenient. Instead, Marg "quick-froze" all of our tomatoes and we were able to put off our canning until this past weekend.

There is nothing quite so wonderful as the aroma of simmering tomatoes, peppers, onions, and all of the other ingredients that go into chili.

We worked very hard, but it was worth all of our efforts. We have many jars for our own use, as well as a number of extras for friends and church bazaars.

TUESDAY — OCTOBER 27

M USIC is the art of the prophets, the only art that can calm the agitations of the soul; it is one of the most magnificent and delightful presents God has given us.

—*Martin Luther*

WEDNESDAY — OCTOBER 28

O THOU
Who has given me eyes
To see the light
That fills my room,
Give me the inward vision
To behold Thee in this place.

THURSDAY — OCTOBER 29

I T takes courage to love because love involves the risk of being hurt or disappointed. To love is to suffer with those we love, to feel their failures, their mistakes, and their pain. To love is to feel the anguish of the poor and the dispossessed and to seek remedies for their plight. Only the courageous dare to love.

—*Marie Busch*
Pulpit Digest

FRIDAY — OCTOBER 30

Bill and Phyllis brought the twins over this evening to help carve the Hallowe'en pumpkin. Several days ago Bruce had gone to the library and borrowed a book describing how to carve "award-winning" pumpkins.

This evening, Jenny and Justin were absolutely enthralled as they watched an ordinary pumpkin become a "horrifying witch."

After the candle was placed inside for a test showing and the huge black hat was perched on top of the terrible face, the children declared that it was the scariest pumpkin ever—a complete success!

SATURDAY — OCTOBER 31

It was such fun to see the children this evening. Watching the little ones tentatively holding out their bags while they whispered "trick or treat" brought back memories of my own children on Hallowe'en. These special holidays surely help to keep one feeling young.

November

SUNDAY — NOVEMBER 1

ALMIGHTY God, whose chosen servant Abraham obeyed your call, rejoicing in your promise that in him the family of the earth is blessed—give us faith like his, that in us your promises may be fulfilled; through Jesus Christ our Lord, who lives and reigns with you and the Holy Spirit, One God, now and forever. Amen.

MONDAY — NOVEMBER 2

THE autumn frosts will lie upon the grass
Like bloom on grapes of purple-brown
and gold,
The misted early mornings will be cold;
The little puddles will be roofed with glass.
—*Elinor Wylie*

THE HERITAGE BOOK

MARG and I spent a most interesting afternoon at our local high school. For several years, groups of students have been involved in an anti-drinking-and-driving campaign, and this year a special assembly was held. One of the speakers, an American, made a great impact with the story he told.

Ten years ago, Kevin Tunell, a 17-year-old boy, killed a young woman named Susan Herzog in a drunk driving accident in Fairfax County, Virginia. When his friends had urged him not to drive, Kevin bragged, "Nothing will ever happen to me." But he lost control of his car, and smashed into Susan's Volkswagen. She was pronounced dead at the scene.

After pleading guilty to drunk driving and involuntary manslaughter, he was sentenced to three years probation and one year of community service lecturing on the perils of drinking and driving. He also agreed to send a cheque every week to Susan's parents. The cheque was for just one dollar and he would send it every Friday for eighteen years (Susan's age when she died).

By all appearances, Kevin got off lightly. However, he was found guilty of contempt of court for not paying the one dollar. The guilt he felt every time he had to write Susan's name had become too much to bear.

WEDNESDAY — NOVEMBER 4

LORD, I shall be very busy this day. I may forget thee . . . but do not Thou forget me.

THURSDAY — NOVEMBER 5

FAR away there in the sunshine are my highest aspirations. I may not reach them, but I can look up and see their beauty, believe in them, and try to follow where they lead.

—*Louisa May Alcott*

FRIDAY — NOVEMBER 6

COURAGE does not consist of feeling no fear, but of conquering fear. He is the hero who, seeing the lions on either side, goes straight on, because there his duty lies.

SATURDAY — NOVEMBER 7

IN after-years when you recall
The days of pleasure past,
And think of joyous hours,
And all have flown so fast;

When some forgotten air you hear
Brings back past scenes for thee,
And gently claims your listening ear
Keep one kind thought for me.

—Fred Boyer

SUNDAY — NOVEMBER 8

THIS is a quotation from Paul's letter to his "Son in the Faith," Timothy.

"Keep before you an outline of the sound teaching which you heard from me, living by the faith and the love which are ours in Christ Jesus."

—2 Timothy 1:13

MONDAY — NOVEMBER 9

IT is the ability to take a joke, not make one, which proves you have a sense of humour.

—Max Eastman

THE HERITAGE BOOK

I SPENT some time today remembering a wonderful hockey coach. No, it was not Joe Blake, or Punch Imlach—it was Priscilla Jean Wanless.

Priscilla was a coach with the Milton Girls Hockey Team from 1985-1989. Her daughter Joanne was a player on the team and Priscilla, along with another parent, Bob (Pie) Lee, took on the coaching duties at a time when the girls were in the PeeWee division. It was an interesting match-up of personalities: while Pie was a very outspoken person Priscilla was quiet, yet she was respected whenever she had something to say. Each year, thanks to the dedication and determination of the coaches, the team improved tremendously.

In April of 1989, Priscilla discovered that she had pancreatic cancer. In the final months of her life, Priscilla showed a courage and determination that will be an inspiration to her team for many years. Although Priscilla passed away in July 1989, her spirit stayed with the team through the season and in April of 1990, the Milton Girls Hockey Team, with the letters P.J.W. on their sweaters, proudly skated away with their first ever Provincial Championship Banner!

THE HERITAGE BOOK

Remembrance Day

IF I should die, think only this of me:
That there's some corner of a foreign field
That is forever England. There shall be
In that rich earth a richer dust concealed;
A dust whom England bore, shaped, made
    aware,
Gave, once, her flowers to love, her ways to
    roam;
A body of England's, breathing English air
Washed by the rivers, blest by suns of home.
And think, this heart, all evil shed away,
A pulse in the eternal mind, no less
Gives somewhere back the thoughts by
    England given;
Her sights and sounds; dreams happy as her
    day;
And laughter, learnt of friends, and gentleness,
In hearts at peace, under an English heaven.

                    —Rupert Brooke

Let us all pray that the world shall one day live
all together in peace and harmony.

THE HERITAGE BOOK

YOUTH is not a time of life—it is a state of mind. You are as young as your faith, as old as your doubt; as young as your self-confidence, as old as your fear; as young as your hope, as old as your despair.

MY grandson Marshall called this evening to give me a good chuckle.

"You know, Gran, that we have never believed in bad luck on Friday the 13th, but today was a day that could easily change that.

"I needed to be in court at 9 a.m. this morning so I got up early. A fuse had blown for the hot water tank so I had a very cold shower. Just before leaving, I hugged Bethany and she threw up all over my suit. I changed quickly and headed for the car—it had a flat tire. I took Jamie's car which, as usual, had almost no gas. I rushed into the service station, filled up, and realized that my wallet was in my other suit. The manager said that Jamie could pay him when he changed the flat tire. By now I was very late. I was speeding. Suddenly there were red flashing lights in my mirror. I got a ticket. I arrived late at the courthouse. The judge was not pleased. I lost my case."

SATURDAY — NOVEMBER 14

To watch the sun set in the west without re-
gretting;
To hail its advent in the east—the night forget-
ting;
To have enough to share—to know the joy of
giving;
To thrill with all the sweets of life—is living.

SUNDAY — NOVEMBER 15

THIS was a very special morning at our church. It was the baptism of Jamie and Marshall's baby daughter, Bethany. It was with love and great pride that I heard the minister's voice saying, "We receive this child into Christ's flock, and do sign her with the sign of the Cross, in token that hereafter she shall not be ashamed to confess the faith of Christ crucified, and to fight under his baptism banner against sin, the world, and the devil, and to continue as Christ's faithful soldier and servant unto her life's end."

THE HERITAGE BOOK

As I gazed at the snow-covered branches this morning, I was reminded of these lines of Henry David Thoreau:

I have remembered when the winter came
High in my chamber in the frosty nights,
When in the still light of the cheerful moon,
On every twig and rail and jutting spout,
The icy spears were adding to their length
Against the arrows of the coming sun.

Instead of putting others in their place, put yourself in their place.

You are growing old gracefully when the number of things you can no longer do is roughly equal to the number of things you no longer want to do.

THE HERITAGE BOOK

MY son-in-law Bruce told me about a sign in front of a restaurant that reads, "Now Hiring Fresh Cream Pies." Apparently last week it read, "Now Hiring New Chicken Livers." Sentences that are worded incorrectly can be very amusing. Here are some other examples:

"An investigation found that the employee occasionally slept on duty for almost five years."

"No detail is too small to overlook."

"It is a once in a lifetime opportunity that I hope to repeat many times."

"Your thumb or fingerprint will be taken."

"The cyclist hopes to survive the 2020-mile race through the French countryside and mountains to ride down Paris' eloquent avenue, Champs Elysées."

REMEMBER that "average" is as close to the bottom as it is to the top.

THE HERITAGE BOOK

For several years now doctors have been telling the world what many of us already knew: walking is good for you.

However, if you walk regularly and vigorously it is important to follow some simple rules.

Choose the right shoes. They should be lightweight and well-cushioned, with a shock-absorbing sole. The uppers should be made of breathable material such as leather or nylon mesh. They should also have substantial arch support, and a toe that allows plenty of room.

Maintain good posture. Keep your back erect and eyes ahead and swing your arms back and forth.

Keep a brisk pace using long, even strides, but never walk until you are so tired that you couldn't cover the same distance the next day.

Try to walk at least three times a week (but preferably four) for about twenty minutes each time. Vary your route to make it as enjoyable as possible.

For many of us oldsters, walking may be the only exercise we get. I have found that I feel much better since I've made walking a daily habit. Maybe it could work for you, too!

SUNDAY — NOVEMBER 22

STIR up, we beseech thee, O Lord, the wills of thy faithful people; that they, plenteously bringing forth the fruit of good works, may of thee be plenteously rewarded; through Jesus Christ our Lord.

—The Book of Common Prayer
Collect for the Sunday before Advent

MONDAY — NOVEMBER 23

YESTERDAY marked the anniversary of a date infamous in American history: the assassination in 1963 of John F. Kennedy, 35th President of the United States. I remember well the words from his inaugural address:

"My fellow Americans, ask not what your country can do for you—ask what you can do for your country. My fellow citizens of the world: ask not what America will do for you, but what together we can do for the freedom of man."

TUESDAY — NOVEMBER 24

NEVER return a kindness—pass it on.

THE HERITAGE BOOK

MY daughter Julia enjoys opera very much and it was she who told me this story about one of Canada's most gifted opera stars.

On May 26, 1938, in a small room over a Chinese laundry in downtown Toronto, a baby was born.

Exactly sixteen years later a man walked into a Greek restaurant run by Manny Stratakis, from Crete, and had lunch. When it was time to settle the bill, the man couldn't pay. All he had was a bit of change and two tickets to Maple Leaf Gardens—for the opera. Manny agreed to accept the tickets in payment.

That night in 1954, on her sixteenth birthday, Manny's daughter Stasia got her first taste of opera. The Metropolitan Opera Company, direct from New York, presented "La Bohème" with Renata Tebaldi as Mimi. Stasia Stratakis was enthralled. "That's what I want to do!" Stasia told her parents.

After four years of intensive study, Stasia made her debut at the Toronto Opera Festival—as Mimi in "La Bohème." One year later she was hired by the Met, and a gifted soprano known as Teresa Stratas was on her way.

THE HERITAGE BOOK

B EAUTY pleases the eyes only, sweetness of disposition charms the soul.

—Voltaire

I HOPE you enjoy this poem, "A Mother's Prayer."

Give me patience when little hands
Tug at me with ceaseless small demands.
Give me gentle words and smiling eyes,
And keep my lips from hasty sharp replies,
Let me not in weariness, confusion, or noise
Obscure my vision from life's fleeting joys
That when in years to come my house is still,
Beautiful memories its rooms may fill.

T HE study of God's word, for the purpose of discovering God's will, is the secret discipline which has formed the greatest characters.

—J.W. Alexander

THE HERITAGE BOOK

1st Sunday in Advent

I⊤ came upon a midnight clear,
That glorious song of old,
From angels bending near the earth,
To touch their harps of gold:
Peace on the earth, good will to men
From heaven's all gracious king!
The world in solemn stillness lay
To hear the angels sing.
                              —*Edward Hamilton Sears*

MONDAY — NOVEMBER 30

THE most completely lost of all days is that
on which one has not laughed.
                              —*Sebastien Chamfort*

December

S NOW came last night
I woke to find on iron
Fence and gate a kind of joy,
A feathery, wild thing that
Will take wing.

O magical, enchanting snow!
From other winters long ago,
Come travelling the starry way
Horses and sleigh.

And children wearing sweaters
    bright
And bells that jingle in the
    night
And whiteness settling everywhere
    like angels' hair.

—*Helen F. Dougher*

THE HERITAGE BOOK

MARG and I spent a lovely day in front of a roaring fire, sipping cups of hot tea and writing our Christmas cards.

This is a task I greatly enjoy. Because I feel it is important to keep in touch with old friends (and new), I usually spend a great deal of time writing notes and letters that I hope will make receiving the card a little more special. Something I have never resorted to, although many have, is a photocopied letter. I feel that this type of letter loses the personal touch and takes away from the special nature of a Christmas greeting.

Although it took the whole day long to write my cards, when I finally finished it was with a marvellous feeling of fatigue.

Over the next few weeks I will look forward anxiously to the postman's arrival each day, in anticipation of the cards and letters that good friends will send me in return.

If ever you feel lonely at this time of year, I heartily recommend the Christmas letter cure.

A WELL-KNIT family is one where everybody gives a darn.

FRIDAY — DECEMBER 4

THE quickest way to become an old dog is to stop learning new tricks.

SATURDAY — DECEMBER 5

ONE of my favourite magazines is *Good Housekeeping*. I especially like the December issue because it features prize-winning gingerbread houses that have been selected from entries across North America.

Several years ago, I cut out the recipe for a "little country cottage," but I hadn't the courage to try to make it until today. Phyllis, Marg, and I decided to follow the directions very carefully, step by step, and see if we could come close to the delightful result pictured in the magazine.

As it turned out, it was less difficult than it appeared. Phyllis, who has the patience of a saint, was given the job of "finishing" the window frames, the wreath on the front door, the Christmas garlands, and the other tiny details that neither Marg nor I had the perseverance to deal with.

We now have a beautiful centrepiece for our Christmas table. There is joy in a task done well.

THE HERITAGE BOOK

2nd Sunday in Advent

Once in Royal David city
Stood a lowly cattle shed,
Where a mother laid her baby
In a manger for his bed.
Mary was that mother mild
Jesus Christ the little child.

He came down to earth from heaven
Who is God and Lord of all,
And his shelter was a stable
And his cradle was a stall.
With the poor and mean and lowly
Lived on earth our Saviour holy.
                        —*Cecil Frances Alexander*

THIS time of year is especially difficult for our friends who are shut-ins or invalids. Family and friends are so busy these days that they often miss their regular visits, yet it is often now when their company is most needed and welcomed.

Try to remember the reason for the season and take time to visit with those friends and family to whom it means so much.

TUESDAY — DECEMBER 8

EMPLOY your time in improving yourself by other men's writings so that you shall come easily by what others have laboured hard for.

—Socrates

WEDNESDAY — DECEMBER 9

AS one journeys through life, and the shadows begin to fall eastward, one reaches the solemn conclusion that too much of the world's wisdom is uttered, and too little lived.

—Bob Edwards

THURSDAY — DECEMBER 10

CHARACTER is that which reveals moral purpose, exposing the class of things a man chooses or avoids.

—Aristotle

FRIDAY — DECEMBER 11

SEVERAL young high school students from our area stopped by this evening. This year, as in the past, the students are collecting canned goods and money to assist the needy families in the area. The money goes toward a turkey, vegetables, and fresh fruit to provide a Christmas dinner for each of the families.

I wish that those who often lump all teen-agers under the headings "drug users" or "lovers of horrible music" or "punks" could spend just a few minutes with the young people who were here this evening. They were polite, articulate, and obviously caring individuals doing their best to make a happy Christmas for those less fortunate than themselves.

SATURDAY — DECEMBER 12

FEAR not that thy life shall come to an end, but rather that it shall never have a beginning.

—Cardinal Newman

THE HERITAGE BOOK

3rd Sunday in Advent

HARK! The herald angels sing
Glory to the new-born King
Peace on earth and mercy mild
God and sinners reconciled
Joyful all ye nations rise
Join the triumph of the skies
With angelic hosts proclaim
Christ is born in Bethlehem
Hark, the herald angels sing
Glory to the new-born king.

—Charles Wesley

MONDAY — DECEMBER 14

JUSTIN and Jenny were very excited when they phoned this evening. Today their teacher had helped each student make a "Christmas present" for the wild birds.

The children were given pine cones which they packed with peanut butter and rolled in wild bird seed. They attached a bright red ribbon to each cone so that it could hang from a tree branch in each child's back yard.

The children are so fortunate to have a caring teacher who shows them the joy in the giving of simple gifts.

THE HERITAGE BOOK

IF you have doubt about doing something, ask yourself if you would do it if it were the last hour of your life.

WHEN you can do the common things in life in an uncommon way you will command the attention of the world.
—*George Washington Carver*

REPROVE a friend in secret, but praise him before others.
—*Leonardo da Vinci*

THOSE who think about doing something are usually passed by someone already doing it.

THE HERITAGE BOOK

THE Christmas time of giving can become quite a challenge to one's ingenuity when one lives, as I do, on a fixed income. Expensive gifts are out of the question, but it's amazing how far a few dollars and a lot of imagination will take you.

Several friends and I have come up with a few gift suggestions that can give a lot of pleasure with a minimum of expense.

— to young parents, free babysitting that allows them some special time to themselves
— to friends who live alone, "visit vouchers" that may be redeemed at any time and that allow them to visit with you for a special lunch or dinner
— to friends who have no gardens, some fruit or vegetable preserves
— to young children, a special photo album that includes all kinds of family pictures from as many generations as possible

I'm sure that you have many more ideas.

THE HERITAGE BOOK

4th Sunday in Advent

O COME all ye faithful
Joyful and triumphant,
O come ye, O come ye to Bethlehem.
Come and behold Him,
Born the King of angels.
O come let us adore Him,
O come let us adore Him,
O come let us adore Him,
Christ the Lord.

MONDAY — DECEMBER 21

H ERE is a list of "Priceless Gifts to Give."

To your opponent—tolerance.
To your friend—your heart.
To a child—good example.
To yourself—respect.
To all people—charity.

THE HERITAGE BOOK

TUESDAY — DECEMBER 22

"EVERYTHING happens for the best," we're told. But have you ever noticed that this is only said when bad things happen?

WEDNESDAY — DECEMBER 23

SILENCE is never more golden than when you keep it long enough to get all the facts.

THURSDAY — DECEMBER 24

"CHRISTMAS Eve." Even now, those two words cause my heart to beat a little faster with anticipation.

As a child, I could scarcely walk with both feet on the ground on the night before Christmas. I remember lying in bed with my eyes shut tight for "hours" without falling asleep. My mother, knowing of my excitement, would often come into my room and softly sing carols until I fell asleep.

Tonight I will shut my eyes and in my mind perhaps I'll hear those soft carols again.

Friday — December 25

Christmas Day

> Joy to the world! The Lord is come.
> Let earth receive her King!
> Let every heart prepare Him room
> And heaven and nature sing,
> And heaven and nature sing,
> And heaven and heaven and nature sing,
>
> A very Merry Christmas to you all!

Saturday — December 26

Today is Boxing Day. The name "Boxing Day" is derived from an English tradition: on the day after Christmas, boxes were distributed to churches, and the contents given to those who rendered small services without pay.

Boxing Day as we know it has an entirely new tradition. As my son-in-law Bruce put it, "Boxing Day is the day you pack your gifts in boxes and return them to the store for exchange."

THE HERITAGE BOOK

Sunday — December 27

A NGELS from the realms of glory,
Wing your flight o'er all the earth;
Ye who sang creation's story
Now proclaim Messiah's birth;
Come and worship, come and worship
Worship Christ the new-born King.

Monday — December 28

W ISDOM isn't the acquisition of knowledge. It's knowing which knowledge is worth acquiring.

Tuesday — December 29

I F God hath made this world so fair
Where sin and death abound,
How beautiful beyond compare
Will paradise be found.

—James Montgomery

THE HERITAGE BOOK

THE secret of happiness is to make others believe that they are the cause of it.

OLD One, lie down,
Your journey is done,
Little New Year
Will rise with the sun.
Now you have come to
The foot of the hill,
Lay down your bones,
Old Year, and lie still.

Young One, step out,
Your journey's begun,
Weary Old Year
Makes way for his son.
Now you have started
To climb up the hill,
Put your best foot forward,
New Year, with a will.

—*Eleanor Farjeon*

A Happy and Blessed New Year to You All!